From An Arabic Language Hymnal

Translated Hymns from the Levant

S. K. Haddad

Kingdom Publishers

From an Arabic Language Hymnal
Copyright© S. K. Haddad

All rights reserved. No part of this book may be
reproduced in any form by photocopying or any
electronic or mechanical means, including information
storage or retrieval systems, without permission in
writing from both the copyright owner and the publisher
of the book. The right of S. K. Haddad to be identified as the author of
this work has been asserted by him in
accordance with the Copyright, Designs and Patents Act
1988 and any subsequent amendments thereto.

A catalogue record for this book is available from the
British Library.

ISBN: 978-1-911697-67-1

1st Edition by
Kingdom Publishers,
London, UK.

You can purchase copies of this book from any leading bookstore or
email **contact@kingdompublishers.co.uk**

Dedicated to my dear brother Amin

PREFACE

The Ottoman occupation of Syria lasted four centuries until the end of the First World War. Syria included the provinces of Lebanon and Palestine. During this time the literary Arabic language was in decline until it was revived by the Christians of Syria. The Christians were a majority in Lebanon until recently when the Muslims outnumbered them.

The translated Arabic hymns in this book were taken from Spiritual Hymns for Evangelical Churches and is used by evangelical churches in Lebanon. They were first gathered in 1863 in a volume without musical tunes, and in 1878 with tunes. Later on some hymns were deleted and others added and the first edition of the new volume with tunes was published in 1949. The hymns were composed mainly in the 19th and 20th centuries.

The translated hymns were taken from the book *The Spiritual Songs For Evangelical Churches* that was published by the American Press in Beirut in 1949. A later revised edition was published in 1990, but I used the original version in my translation.

Syria, Lebanon, and Palestine were one country of Greater Syria, under the rule of the Ottoman Turks for 4 centuries until the end of the First World War. Lebanon and Palestine were provinces of Greater Syria. Arabic culture was in decline and became neglected until it was revived by the Lebanese, Syrian and Palestinian Christians of the 19th and early 20th centuries who were in the forefront of the Arabic literary revival. Many of them then resided in Egypt. It is not surprising that most of the hymns in the hymnal were written by Lebanese, Syrian and Palestinian Christians, in the second half of the 19th century up tothe middle of the 20th.

The title of the book is, From the Arabic language Hymnal, not, from The Arabic Hymnal. It is a hymnal in the Arabic language, but is not a hymnal of the Arabs. There is a common misconception that all Arabic speaking peoples are Arabs. This is the same as saying that all English speaking peoples are English or all Portuguese or Spanish speaking peoples are Portuguese or Spaniards. The Arabs are the indigenous inhabitants of Arabia and the Gulf. The Lebanese people are the descendants of the ancient Canaanites, commonly known as Phoenicians. They were influenced by and intermingled throughout the ages with empire builders, such as the Akkadians, Egyptians, Assyrians, Babylonians, Persian, Greeks, Romans (Byzantine), Arabs, and Turks. The Arab conquest of Lebanon was in the 7th century A.D. Because the Aramaic language, the mother of all Semitic languages was spoken by the Lebanese, it was easy for the conquered people to adopt the language of their conquerors. Eventually, all the conquered peoples in the Middle East and North Africa adopted the Arabic language, especially because they adopted Islam, the religion of the Arabs. That was the process of Arabization of the Middle East and North Africa, and the majority today, who are ethnically mixed, are erroneously regarded as Arabs. The Lebanese Christians lived mainly in the mountains and escaped Islamization. They are not Arabs, nor are the "Berbers of North Africa" of whom came St. Augustine and probably Tertullian, and who should be properly called the Amazigh. The ethnically mixed people of Egypt are descendants of Pharaonic Egypt.

I used rhymes in the translation in the same manner as they appear in the Arabic language hymn book. All the lines of a verse may rhyme, or the first with the third and the second with the fourth, or other variants. The Arabic language is such that two or three words may be composed of eight or more syllables. It is not possible to translate them into English with two or three words and retain the same number of syllables and meaning. I managed this without changing what the verses say: the added words being complementary to the original meaning. The result is a fairly accurate translation of these superb Arabic language hymns.

I translated a fraction of the whole, paying special attention to hymns that magnify God and the work of our Lord Jesus Christ. Many hymns are personal in the sense that the author wrote of the troubles and sorrows and fears of this life and how he placed his trust in his Lord who was able to deliver him.

A number of hymns in the Arabic language hymnal are translations of English hymns. I translated 25 hymns of these before realizing my error, but then left them out. Some may have escaped me, but I am not aware of any.

The pronunciation of the letter *G* in names, such as al-Yazigi or Girgis or Gamal is like that in Giant in English, with the absence of the hidden *D* such as is found in General, pronounced as Dgeneral. It is not like that in Gift. The Egyptians pronounce the letter *G* as in Gift, that is, as a Gimmel in the Hebrew language, but the Arabic pronunciation is as in Giant. The pronunciation of *S* in names, and surnames, such as ar-Rasi, is like that in the Sun and not a Z as in Praise.

Many of the personal names have a prolonged second syllable and I spelt them in a manner to portray this. Ameen is commonly spelt, Amin, and Ibraheem, as Ibrahim. My own name Saleem was erroneously spelt Salim on my birth certificate, My middle name, which is my father's name, is mis-spelt as Khalil. My use of the double *e* gives a more accurate spelling of the names than the use of the letter *i*.

I am indebted to Dr. Eirwen Joy Davies for helping me to match the words to the tunes. It was not possible in some cases to do so and she gave me alternative tunes. At times I had to find alternative words to fit the tune. Unfortunately, I do not read music and needed Dr Davies's help.

FROM THE ARABIC LANGUAGE HYMNAL

1 | Tune: Trinity, 6 & 4s.

To the merciful One,
World's Creator and Sun,
We offer praise;
The Father, Creator,
The Son our Redeemer,
The Spirit, life giver,
We bless and praise.

O redemption's Author,
Look from Heaven over
Each one and all.
Protect us from our foes
And from destruction's throes
And with guidance repose
Each waiting soul.

O Word of God, most fair,
O Hearer of our prayer,
O Forgiver,
Give us the Father's joy,
Your Spirit to enjoy11

And redemption employ
O Conqueror.

O Spirit of our God,
Source of life and of blood,
O mighty One,
Cover our failures now,
Cleanse our hearts and endow
Purity as we bow,
O holy One.

People, kneel and worship
The Creator's kingship,
The Eternal.
To Him who is mighty,
Our ancient Trinity,
Praise be with amity
Sempiternal.

Anonymous.

2 | Tune: Secret Prayer, C.M., 8,6. Chorus, 7s.

Blessed be that majesty who
Created each being;
Blessed be my Redeemer too
Who bled for me, dying.

Chorus
All glory to God on high,
Creatures, give praise to the Lamb,
People, praise Him, magnify,
He is Lord, the great I AM.

And the loud song of the redeemed
Is pleasant to my ear
Of Jesus, worthy and esteemed
Who died for me down here.

I love to sing the wisdom and
Grandeur beyond degree,
Of man's Creator in each land,
Of mountain and of tree.

I hear the songs of angels there
As they worship the King,
Their tune fills the heavens and air
As they praise Him and sing.

As'ad ash-Shadoodi (1826-1906).

3 | Tune: Jesus died for you, C.M.
Chorus: 5,5,8,6.

Bow down to our Creator Lord:
Redeemer dignified,
Worship none other nor accord:
He only is our guide.

Chorus
Merciful and kind;
Worlds of every kind
Were made by Him,
But praise Him more:
He has redeemed mankind.

For this is David's son who came
With the good news for all;
His works bore witness to His name
That He is Lord of all.

The prophets of long time ago
Told of His matchless worth;
The saints blessed Him with wondrous awe
Before He came to earth.

His words were such that hearts would melt,
Would crumple or adore
And eyes that saw His beauty felt
Their youthfulness once more.

Ibraaheem Sarkees (1837-1885).

4 | Tune: Old Hundredth, L.M., 8s.

To God who from eternity
Is Father, Son, Holy Spirit,
The dwellers in Heaven and earth
Ascribe worthy endless merit.

And all who are under the sky
Send forth to the Creator praise,
While thanks from every mouth is heard
To Christ our Lord, now and always.

His mercy does not end at all,
His word is truth for all to see
And in our land His praise remains
For all time and eternity.

O God, exalted and most high,
Our gracious Master and our Lord,
How glorious is Your splendid name
Above our homeland and seaboard!

Your throne, above all thrones of men,
Above all ranks, and stands sublime,
A steadfast throne of majesty
Through the ages and beyond time.

O Lord of hosts, how beautiful
Must be Your holy dwelling place;
Our hearts and souls, with eagerness,
Yearn to be there to see Your face.

With much pity and with much grace
Your precious salvation has been
Broadcast with faithfulness to men
So that the truth was heard and seen.

Your mercy exceeds and outweighs
All the good things life can afford
And everything bears witness to
The fact that You are God the Lord.

Naseef al-Yazigi (1800-1871).

5 | Tune: Rivaulx, L.M., 8s.

We praise him who fills all in all,
The living One, eternal, high,
Our Lord of hosts to whom we call,
Mighty Creator, ever nigh.

O Father, who hears those who call,
Accept your children who believe;
Before Your throne we kneel and fall
In worship as to you we cleave.

O sole Saviour, to you we owe
Our redemption, costly and dear;
Let a deep love within us grow
As time goes by from year to year.

O mighty Spirit, come and prove
Our hearts and cleanse them from within;
No other helper can remove
Sins and the blemishes of sin.

To God the Father and the Son
And Spirit we united bow,
To the living, answering One
Whom, with great love, we worship now.

George Ford (1851-1928).

6 | Tune: Canonbury, L.M., 8s.

Glory to God the mighty One,
The Lord of hosts eternally;
Praise to His noble name be done
By all His creatures readily.

We render thanks and lasting praise
To the eternal God who shows
Wonderful mercy in His ways
And boundless grace that overflows.

Almighty Lord, we only need
Your presence and redemptive grace,
Our hearts long for, while our souls plead
Your favour on us and our race.

Naseem al-Hilo (1868-1951).

7 | Tune: Shipston, 8&7.

Praise the Lord, praise him mightily
And publicly state His deeds;
Sing to him, oh sing heartily,
Magnify His works indeed.

Call upon His most holy name,
He grants our souls life and light;
Seek him who is ever the same,
The God of strength and of might.

The judge of earth and of Heaven,
He will not ever forget
The covenant He has given
With the promises He set.

For His people receive showers:
Riches on the path they tread,
Therefore sing His praises all hours,
Hallelujah to our Head.

Naseef al-Yazigi (1800-1871).

8 | Tune: State Street, S.M., 6&8.

His the authority,
Possessor of all things,
So praise him with all purity
For the favours He brings.

Rise and worship before
His throne with awe and fear,
The Creator whom we adore
Who made worlds far and near.

Listen to Him fully,
His people on this earth,
Submit to Him obediently
Acknowledging his worth.

Give to the Father praise,
Magnify the Son,
Glorify the Spirit always,
Our God the Three in One.

Naseef al-Yazigi (1800-1871).

9 | Tune: Oak, 6,4,6,4,6,7,6,4. *

My soul, arise and praise
The Lord of Heaven,
As long as you remain
Let praise be given;
Put not your hope and trust
In lords or princes who must
Leave their glory to dust
And destruction.

He who takes refuge in
Our God is blest,
The God of our nation,
A fort of rest
And a mighty helper
And creation's Creator
And a faithful shelter,
Life's Lord and quest.

He is the One who gives
Vengeance in kind
Upon the oppressors
Of humankind.
He feeds the hungry poor
And redeems the prisoner,

Removes the night to cure
Eyes that are blind.

My Lord supports all those
Whose troubles soar,
Loves those that fear His name
And yet adore;
Punishes guilty ones,
Judging the cause of orphans
While His kingdom still runs
For evermore.

As'ad ash-Shadoodi (1826-1906).

10 | Tune: Azmon C.M., 8&6.

Thank God whose favour overflows
Like a vast swelling sea,
Waters the earth of His bounty
With rain on plant and tree.

All mortals are His creation
And worlds were in His plan
And by sprinkling the night with stars
Made glad the heart of man.

All things that we live by come from
His favour in each case;
Let us always thank Him and praise
The greatness of His grace.

We thank you Lord for all the gifts
That You did freely give,
Of money, health and other things
That we may grow and live.

So, for Your goodness, accept, Lord
Hearts full of sincere love
And deep feelings of gratitude
For Your gifts from above.

Ameen Faris (1867-1936).

11 | Tune: St. Albans. 11s.

O my Soul, arise and bless the Lord your God
Who wears the light in Heaven, a robe of white,
Who spreads the firmaments like tents in the sky
While waters roof the vast regions in the height.

He walks upon the spreading wings of the wind
And rides upon the clouds, in their dark attire,
Who made His angels spirits to do His will
And obedient ministers of flaming fire.

The sun has risen in the morning, the beasts
Gather their armies to seek their desired food
And people rise and hurry, each to his work:
The Creator's wisdom is both great and good.

All hope that You will give them their sustenance
In its season, O generous and kind Lord;
All are filled with the goodness that You bestow
On Your creatures as You spread Your hands abroad.

My duty is to thank the Lord all my days
And sing His praise for favours He loves to give;
The Lord finds pleasure in my words and my song:
I rejoice in my God as long as I live.

Naseef al-Yazigi (1800-1871).

12 | Tune: Jesus loves the little children, 8s & 7s.

Thanking your holy name, our theme
Shall be of generous grace;
In mercy you chose to redeem
Our rebellious human race;
Accepted the cross where You died,
Drank God's cup of displeasure,
Justice and mercy satisfied:
A wonder without measure.

The love of God appeared when He
Called us beyond human strife:
People of earth, now come to me
And drink the water of life.
What we received of God's good hand
Was through Your name, wondrous One,
God said of You when in our land:
You are my beloved Son.

The spring of life, the great giver,
The choicest of all abroad,
Most holy Maker, forgiver,
Our upright and faithful Lord.

Therefore, with passionate ardour
And with lasting happiness,
To Your Holy name we offer,
Noble Lord, our thankfulness.

Saleem Kassab (1842-1907).

13 | Tune: Dedham, C.M., 8 & 6.

I pray with thanks most readily
To You in the morning,
So hear my cry and that early,
Answer my heart's longing.

You are a righteous God of grace,
You cannot accept sin;
The guilty draws near to Your face,
Repentant and drawn in.

You dislike transgressors, O God,
Who lie and go astray;
You hate the wicked who shed blood,
Deceit and craft their way.

Lord, let Your mercy protect me,
Prostrate I humbly bow,
Wishing most urgently to see
Your gracious presence now.

Your justice is upright and wise,
Guide me to it each day;
Make plain my path and set my eyes
Upon the narrow way.

Naseef al-Yazigi (1800-1871).

14 | Tune: Melita, L.M., 8s.*

O Father, merciful and good,
The source of every light that shines,
My heart draws near with gratitude
And for Your noble presence pines;
O Watcher over me by night,
Safeguard me also by daylight.

O Jesus, Lord, bright morning star,
My guiding light throughout my days,
I offer thanks for what You are
And humbly follow all Your ways;
O righteous Sun, my joy Your smile,
Shine in the night of my exile.

Holy Spirit, bright light of life,
The light of being from the start,
Grant me your blessings, wide and rife,
While I kneel sanctify my heart;
Eternal Spirit, protect me,
My body, soul and spirit, three.

Isbir Doomit (- 1914).

15 | Tune: He leadeth me, L.M., 8s, with chorus.
Truro, 5 verses, no chorus.

O my Soul, rise up hurriedly,
Lo, the morning sun has risen,
Put laziness by, rapidly,
Seek the righteous Lord of Heaven.

Chorus
O Lord who gave the sun to me
To cancel the night set within,
Shine with Your clear light upon me,
Erase the darkness of my sin.

O Lord, ordain the path I tread
And oversee my wayward heart,
Fill it with a spirit instead,
Clean, meek and pure in every part.

And let my strength and thoughts and mind
And every word and work and deed
Revert, O Lord of all mankind,
To Your glory, august indeed.

When the time to depart comes round
From this transient land where I roam,
May I then a dweller be found
Lord, in that everlasting home.

Dawood Qurban (1868-1935).

16 | Tune: St. George's, Windsor, 7s,D.

Behold, morning has appeared,
It is the time to arise
And the darkness disappeared,
The light of peace filled the skies;
The splendid sun is awake
With its brilliance yet again;
Sent its radiance at daybreak
Above hill, mountain and plain.

And the sky gave a big smile
With beauty that would amaze
And the lands sang a long while
The glorious Creator's praise
And I, Master, lift my heart
To You, ruler of all lands,
Spreading out my hands apart
In worship between Your hands.

With reverence I bow and kneel
To You, mighty Lord, who knows
The thanks when I wake and feel
Your bounty that overflows.
You kept me safe and secure
Under the curtains of night

Then woke me up, fresh and sure
Of peace when I meet the light.

My desire, You freely gave
The morning light this new day;
For Your presence I do crave,
Guide me and prosper my way.
Consider the work I do
On this day and bless it all,
Keep my feet, let me eschew
All wrong, O Lord, lest I fall.

Sulaiman Doomit (- 1901).

17 | Tune: St. Ignatius, L.M., 8s.

The light of morn in eastern skies
Shone on my eye to quell the night
O Sun of righteousness, arise
Toward me with Your mercy's light.

I offered to the Ancient Truth
My sacrifice of praise anew;
I weep for my grave sin, forsooth
And for God's Son's mercy I sue.

When work is done the day will close
And I lie down seeking my rest,
Be my keeper in my repose
And let my sleep at night be blest.

But should the sun of my life set,
Be my sun with your brilliant face;
Let not salvation's Light forget
My soul, and bless my resting place.

Anonymous

18 | Tune: Bavaria, 8,7,8,7, Double
Brudergemeinde, 8s & 7s.

Dear Lord, grant us this eventide
A blessing before we rest;
Grant our hearts peace, become our guide,
Chase the darkness from our breast.
O Lord, we have sinned against You,
Walked in our iniquity,
Save and purify us anew,
Cleanse our shame and have pity.

Come, deliver us from all ill,
Our dear Lord, when we lie down,
Guard us and watch over us still,
O man's Saviour of renown.
You are able and Almighty,
Your eyes slumber not nor sleep,
Taking care of weak and mighty
When disasters rage or creep.

If some illness strikes me at night
Or horrendous thing draws nigh,
O my Joy, comfort me outright,
Heal my soul, healer on high,

Then refresh me with your kindness
When the morning shows its face,
Fill my heart with joy and gladness
Granting me favour and grace.

As'ad ash-Shadoodi (1826-1906).

19 | Tune: Evening Praise, 7,7,7,7,4.

When the day's sun goes to sleep
From the sky of my vain world,
Be my light, guide me and keep
My steps to the after world
In my darkness.

Chorus
Oh, the light, the light, the light
Dispels the dark,
I see the Redeemer's light
Leading men to the soul's ark
Toward the cross.

When life's sunset falls on me
In death, soul, do not cower:
That awful darkness will be
Made by God's peace in that hour
My heart's delight.

No setting befalls the Sun
Of righteousness as He brings
Healing till all ill is gone
Through His all protective wings

From my ill plight.

My Lord my guardian is great,
Be gone trouble, be gone fret,
His brightness will not abate
And His face will never set
Out of my sight.

Wadee' al-Hajjar (1905-1978).

20 | Tune: Sabbath, 7s.

The Lord has brought us in peace
To a day that He has blest
To worship and seek His aid
And mighty blessings request.
Oh, what a wonderful day:
Symbol of eternal rest.

As we seek Your favour through
Our beloved Saviour's name,
Show us the face of delight,
Removing our sin and blame
And give us rest from the stress
Of our world of sinful shame.

Let all those assembled feel
The Lord's presence with us now;
Let Your glory be revealed
As we bend our heads and bow
And taste of that purer supper
Bought by Your sad wounded brow.

Your countenance gives comfort
And guidance for those who stay

And an increase of blessings
That cure the soul on that day
And thus we see that Heaven
Bestows its joys on our way.

Anonymous.

21 | Tune:Benevento, 7s.

The sun has travelled with us
To the end of the old year;
Some souls have left the roadway,
We shall not meet with them here,
And went to eternity
Having completed their span,
But we remained after them
For a season in God's plan.

Like trembling of the lightning
That emerged and left no trace,
Our days have run too swiftly
Decreasing the human race;
Our souls were plucked out by God
From danger's valley and face;
All that is under heaven
Like a dream passes apace.

And now that You have kept us
To see this new year on time,
Let Your own garden flourish
With blessings, perfect and prime;
O Sun, rise in our region
From Your high Heaven sublime

And make this New Year for us
Lovelier than the foretime.

Accept the thanks we offer
And pardon us for the past,
Then grant us your benefits
To hold our piety fast.
Bless us with the Saviour's love
And with mercy that will last
Our lives in this fading world
Then take us to homes that last.

Naseef al-Yazigi (1800-1871).

22 | Tune: Sawley, C.M., 8,6,8,6.

I love to distance myself from
Life's troubles our days bring
And spend my hours in the worship
Of my God, the great king.

I love to pour out, when alone,
My grief, distress and hurt
And tears of deep repentance to
The cleaner of my dirt.

I remember a mercy gone
And with verve ask for more,
Lay my sorrow on my Saviour,
The One whom I adore.

I see by faith the high dwellings
Of my Lord standing clear,
Hoping than one day I shall win
The honour to be there.

And when I travel from these lands
Of trouble and of care
I shall gain in His paradise
The utmost pleasure there.

Saleem Abdul-Ahad (- 1960).

23 | Tune: Bless me now, 7s.

Faithful Shepherd, hear our prayer,
O most loving to the sheep,
Keep us always in your care
With compassion, tender, deep.

Chorus
Faithful Shepherd, hear our prayer,
Keep us always in Your care.

With Your awesome visage fill
Hearts with godliness made whole
Giving from Your goodness still
Food to satisfy the soul.

Then accompany Your word
With life wherever it falls,
Strengthen Your purchase who heard
To shun doctrines, new and false.

We confessed with a full heart
Your free gifts, great and sublime,
Grant to us as we depart
Fullness of blessing each time.

Fountain of each blessed gift,
Generous Master always,
We humbly thank You and lift
Our hearts in permanent praise.

As'ad ash-Shadoodi (1826-1906).

24 | Tune: Hamburg, L.M., 8s.

God is a Spirit of great might
And formed all things in every part
And knows all things however slight,
Sees the intentions of the heart.

Deceitful worship never scored,
But with craftiness is allied,
Nor is the false person ignored
Though in cunning he tries to hide.

The hypocrite looks to the sky,
His knees bow down toward the earth
And God is Lord of truth whose eye
Sees and rejects prayers of no worth.

Vainly we raise our voices high
Standing upright with a clear show
When we never bother to try
To lift our souls that stay below.

Lord, guide me to worship you now
With a pure heart open for grace,
Say, take the blessing I endow
As you rise up to seek My face.

Naseef al-Yazigi (1800-1871).

25 | Tune: Jesus, Thy Name I love, 6,6,4,6,6,4.

There is no sweeter name
On earth or Heaven the same
Like my Jesus.
Of all men that are nigh
Or those who dwell on high,
I only seek and sigh
For my Jesus.

You have bought me for good
With Your most precious blood
My Lord Jesus.
For you, by love so great
And mercy's open gate
Redeemed my sinful state
My Lord Jesus.

You are my hiding-place,
Source of favour and grace,
My Lord Jesus,
Therefore I do not fear
Evil or ruin here
As long as You are near
My Lord Jesus.

My heart will sing and laud
The return of the Lord,
My Lord Jesus.
With utmost happiness
For evermore, no less,
I shall see Him and bless
My Lord Jesus.

Anonymous.

26 | Tune: Rest, L.M., 8s.

Your eye, O great exalted Lord,
Pierces the dark veils of the night
And every secret we may hoard
Is fully exposed to Your sight.

All deeds, however small they look,
All word we think, we hide or say
Are clearly written in Your book
To be revealed at the last day.

So will the sins that I have done
Be apparent to all who see
When Heaven's hosts and earth's, each one
Hear of my shame when around me?

O Lord, I do not dare at all
Lift up my eye from shame so great,
Forgive my sins, erase them all
Before the coming of that date.

Let my soul fear and turn aside
From evil thoughts and wrong within,
You see and hear all things inside
And count each transgression and sin.

Anonymous.

27 | Tune: Worthing, L.M.

Wish I could settle at the feet
Of Christ my Lord throughout my days
Hearing the most loved One repeat
His truthful words in pleasant ways.

And when this earth will hide from me
And I go home beyond the sky,
Can there in all creation be
Any like Him who dwells on high?

The life I relish to be in
Has love, and repentance that shows
And firm rejection of all sin,
Abundant peace that overflows.

I will spend days that remain
Casting from me all sin and strife
Until my kind Lord lets me gain
Great joy and everlasting life.

Nasee al-Yazigi (1800-1871).

28 | Tune: Halley, L. M., 8.

O Jesus, Lord of peace, see how
We reverently kneel down and bow
Hoping that You will guide us now,
So hear our plea, O Lord Jesus.

Let us, as true believers, pray
To the Father through You this day
And pity us in every way
And hear our plea, O Lord Jesus.

If there is in life any snare
That keeps us from coming in prayer
Remove it, O God, since You care
And hear our plea, O Lord Jesus.

If doubts assail us and enthral
That you will not answer our call,
Cast them from us, Lord over all
And hear our plea, O Lord Jesus.

Naseem al-Hilo (1868-1951)

29 | Tune: Clarion, 8,7,8,7.

I have a book from my Lord God,
A treasure that bids my night
To gather from its brightness light:
Nothing is like it in sight.

It instructs me when my feet stray,
Shines its guiding light for me,
Shows me how my Redeemer Lord
By His free grace ransomed me.

It leads me and keeps me lowly
In the straight and truthful way,
Expels from me by God's Spirit
Hells terrors that once held sway.

My sharp sword on the day I die,
With it I can conquer death
And fearlessly face the damned one
Triumphant at my last breath.

As'ad ash-Shadoodi (1826-1906).

30 | Tune: Send forth the Bible, 11s.
Kingsley, 11s.

The words of the Lord fill the heart with gladness,
Sweet as the honeycomb, what taste they impart!
The nourishment of bones, they remove sadness,
A potent medicine for the wounded heart.

The word of the wise One that raise up the lame
Are comfort for sad souls, protecting from snares,
The clothes of righteousness, the yoke of Christ's name
And rest for the weary, removing all cares.

The words of the bright One dispel the dark night,
Transform all the ignorant and make them wise,
A guide to the lost and to nations a light,
Showing the way to heaven's eternal prize.

The words of the wise One: riches to the poor,
A storehouse of good and a treasure too great,
A lamp to the seeing, to blind eyes the cure,
A tower of joy with impregnable gate.

Yowakeem ar-Rasi (- 1916).

31 | Tune: St. Agnes C.M., 8,6,8,6.

The universe is but a page
Open for all to read,
It bids us see at every stage
God's great wisdom indeed.

Existence tells its wonders with
The words of the Sublime,
They witness to His might forthwith
Until the end of time.

All His creatures exist and live
Only by His command,
His watchful eye scans all to give
His care in every land.

His blessing, like dew that graces
The heights of Lebanon
Gives life, heals souls and embraces
The hearts and minds anon.

To His name all nations and kings
And Heaven's host give praise
And earth with its created things
Prostrates itself always.

O Lord, You gave the grace to me
To sight Your wondrous deeds,
Now give my soul by faith to see
Your face while life proceeds.

Saleem Abdul-Ahad (- 1960).

32 | Tune: Helmsley, 8,7,8,7,4,7.

He shall come, our faithful Saviour
In the clouds without a haze,
Angels and righteous sons round Him,
All His children singing praise;
Praise, oh, praise Him,
Believers, your voices raise.

He shall come from His high glory
In the clouds with no rainbow
And the eyes of all shall see Him,
Should they be lover or foe;
Glorify Him,
He is the kind Lord we know.

He shall come from highest Heaven
To judge all men, far and near
And the living shall be crowding
The sleeping in every sphere;
O my great God,
Your judgment is just and clear.

What a day when the Beloved
Will come back for us to see,

He, who by His blood redeemed us,
Accepting shame on the tree;
O our Helper,
You are every good to me.

Ibraaheem Sarkees (1837-1885).

33 | Tune: Marching, 8,7,8,7.
Parting Hymn, 8,7,8,7.

Christ shall come, His promise keeping,
Wait, my soul, throw gloom away;
Should you in the grave be sleeping,
Your dark night will turn to day.

Be exalted and rejoicing,
Let nothing your gladness thwart,
Fear not the moment of passing:
The crossing will be too short.

On that famous day you will see
The wondrous bright morning star,
Your deep groaning will end and be
With your weeping flung afar.

In high spheres you will be springing
To your beloved, your goal
And with the angels gladly singing
When your sad heart is made whole.

Antone Badr (-)

34 | Tune: Abridge, C.M., 8,6,8,6.

Believers have waited too long
For their Saviour's return,
Their eager hearts constantly long
And their spirits still yearn.

We humbly lift our voice to You,
In prayer we are near,
Source of salvation, wholly true,
Come, wipe our every tear.

You stayed with us by Your Spirit,
Therefore we dare draw nigh,
Hear us as we plead your merit,
Generous Lord, we cry.

Oh, what a wonderful day when
In person you appear
And we see You and rejoice then
When You are with us here.

O Desire of every nation,
Star of the world, most bright,
Shine forth from your highest station
And come to us outright.

Hurry, Lord Jesus, come, return
With all authority
And over all let your just reign
Glisten with purity.

Sulaiman Doomit (- 1901).

35 | Tune: Lahee (Nativity), C.M., 8,6,8,6.

Lo! Christ comes and rather quickly,
The whole land shall rejoice;
Prepare your heart to be His throne
And praise Him with your voice.

He comes, a glorious conqueror
Confirming victory,
Destroying His enemy's gates
To set the prisoners free.

He comes with a light most brilliant
With healing to blind eyes
That they may see Heaven's bright light
Blazing through shining skies.

He comes giving sick souls healing
To the broken a cure;
His grace covers all of mankind
And enriches the poor.

Shouts of joy shall cry, Hosanna
When He comes in glory;
Voices ring with praise in Heaven
Re-telling His story.

Ibraaheem Baz al-Haddad (- 1923).

36 | Tune: Safe in the Promised Land, L.M., 8s.

O nations of the earth, arise
And seek the house of peace and joy
Before the time comes with surprise
When deep regret will have no ploy.

When the trumpets sound lie thunder,
Come, O Hearers, the heavens break,
See the living walk with wonder
But not before the dead awake.

The scattered dead, some by drowning,
Be they the greatest or the least,
Snatched from vessels, or meat browning
For hungry vulture or wild beast.

It is a dreadful day wherein
The elements dissolve away
While the great Judge will judge each sin
And secrets are exposed that day.

Evildoers duly perish,
The righteous are called to a man:
Receive the kingdom you cherish
Prepared before the world began.

Murad al-Haddad (-).

37 | Tune: Herald Angels, 8,7,8,7,8,7,8,7.

The host of Heaven were singing
To the shepherds in the night
With good news that they were bringing
That salvation was in sight,
Saying, glory in the highest
And on earth peace to mankind
And praise our God from east to west
When joy shall fill hearts once blind.

Hear the tunes of sweet thanksgiving
From the host approaching nigh
With harps that sound almost living
Singing, praise the Lord on high,
For today the Christ has been born
And in a manger was laid:
His firm kingdom cannot be torn,
Lasts for ever, will not fade.

He left His glory and praises
And the sweet hymns of the pure,
Now His sun shines high and blazes
Bringing with its wings the cure.

Rise, O creatures, with contrition,
Raise your voices with accord
For He pardons all transgression,
Our Redeemer, Christ the Lord.

Mitri al-Haddad (- 1910).

38 | Tune: Bearnaise Carol, 8,7,8,7,8,7,8,7.

A sound rang forth in the highest,
What has caused this mystery?
Why do angels raise their voices
With the hymns of victory?
All of them sing forth in glory
Joyous tunes as they gather,
A great wonder appeared to us:
God's mercy, the forgiver.

O ye Shepherds, rise and behold
Now the glorious Lord, a child,
Has become a helpless baby,
Like a slave, lowly and mild.
Glorify Him, Hallelujah,
Glorify Him in the heights,
Glorify Him, Hallelujah,
He is man's Saviour by right.

Peace shall now abide upon earth
And joys to mankind appear
For the great Redeemer has come,
The awaited Christ is here.
Let the sound ring forth for ever
With lyres, golden as the morn,

Hallelujah, He redeemed us,
Righteousness in us is born.

The Redeemer was born humbly,
Yet he is God's Christ, the Lord;
Let earth and Heaven give praises
To His lofty name abroad,
So receive Him who has been called
Of our God, noble and kind,
Yes, has been called Prophet and King
And High Priest, unique in kind.

Come, O Sinners, he is faithful,
Know the Shepherd ardently,
Let His name be your desired hope,
Worship Him obediently.
Whosoever tastes His pleasures
And sees His resplendent light
Shall sing to God, Hallelujah,
Hallelujah in the heights.

Yowakeem ar-Rasi (- 1916).

39 | Tune: Dix, 7s.

Like the bright star that guided
The wise men who travelled on
Till the manger was sighted
As the star above them shone,
Grant to those who lose the way
The bright morning star today.

As they worshipped with favour
The child Jesus, wholesome boy,
And they knelt with much fervour
Adoring Him with pure joy,
May each sinner, like them seek
His mercy who helps the weak.

As they offered frankincense,
Gave Him myrrh and precious gold,
May we like them, now and hence
Give Him all we have and hold,
Thank Him, as we give our days,
For His kind and gracious ways.

Our Lord, grant that we may tread
The straight path and narrow way

That at last we may be led
Up to Heaven, there to stay,
Where the stars no longer guide
And the clouds no longer glide.

No star or sun ever yet
Held such great rank in the sky;
The righteous Sun will not set,
He is Lord, exalted high
So to our Lord Christ we raise,
Now and ever, hearty praise.

Ibraaheem Baz al-Haddad (-1923).

40 | Tune: St. Louis, 8,6,8,6,8,6,8,6.

Upon the hills of Bethlehem
A planet blazed its light,
It brightness clothed the darkness with
A robe of brilliant light.
Do the celestial spheres know that
Light from heaven's ranger
Reflects the light of redemption
In a lowly manger?

Peace has risen in Bethlehem
To the nations of mankind,
Carried by His wonderful birth
In darkness of the blind.
Let people rejoice in the birth
Of the mighty stranger,
Let all men kneel before the child
In the lowly manger.

If hurricanes storm upon us
Storms of hardship and toil
And calamities cover us
With hope lost in the spoil,
Then the high planet's cheerful face
Dispels signs of danger,

Revealing His bright resplendence
In a lowly manger.

Look how it points above the hills
To immortality:
The liberator came to free
All in reality,
His power and His sublime might,
Famous love and grandeur,
His glorious purity, are all
In the lowly manger.

Anees al-Maqdisi (1885-1977).

41 | Tune: Father, forgive them, L.M., 8s. Melita, 8s.

Jesus, my Saviour, wondrous One
Died on the cross, God's only Son
And vanquished death, its terror gone,
Hear that loved One, almost undone,
Cry for those who came together
For His blood, Father, forgive them.

His wounds that flooded from that height
Grant me pardon and inner sight,
Support my weakness in the fight
That I may do the good and right.
Oh, the prayer for foes that gather,
O My Father, do forgive them.

On Golgotha He made us free
From sin, the Lord of all that be,
And after roaming the dark sea,
To peaceful havens He brought me.
While I live I recall His prayer,
O My Father, do forgive them.

George Khoory (b. 1901).

42 | Tune: Expostulations, 11s.

Jesus, you obeyed Your Father's instruction,
Committing Your spirit between His hands when
By death You saved the captives of destruction
And clothed them with the robe of righteousness then.

You gave Yourself to me, lost in ignorance,
Bore the full weight of man's sin through history,
Triumphed over death after much endurance
And rose to receive the crown of victory.

Assist me when despondency comes in sight
And the army of darkness camps around me
And grant Your peace to sustain me, while Your light
Scatters the dark clouds till they scatter and flee.

Turn my eyes towards Your cross with affection
When I come to die, and hold my weary head,
Finish my salvation through Your redemption
And take me to You, Master, when I am dead.

Saleem Abdul-Ahad (- 1960).

43 | Tune: Angelus, L.M., 8s.
L.M., Double 8s.

It is finished, the Lord had said
As He bowed down his head and died;
The time of victory and war
Has finished and the blood has dried.

Finished, all that the prophets said
Throughout the ages of the past,
We have what has not been given
To king, or prophet, or outcast.

It is finished, O Son of God,
You conquered and ruled over all,
We see with sadness that we live
By virtue of your death and gall.

So let us hear the sound that gives
The greatest joy and happiness
Whose echo shall be heard on earth
And in Heaven in its fulness.

Julees Farti (-).

44 | Tune: Blumenthal, 7s, Double.
Redhead 47, 7s.

The Saviour was hung up high
On a cross and insulted,
Bore the scorn and willed to die
Though Lord of all, exalted.

The soldiers came to deride
With the mob's elders and chief;
Before blood poured from His side,
They gave Him myrrh for relief.

He gave up the ghost and died
For transgressors born to strife,
Creation's King crucified
While being the Lord of life!

The temple's curtain was torn,
The graves' portals were scattered,
The sun was as if not born
And the dumb rocks were shattered.

The spring of life to dead bones
Was placed in a tomb like men;

Like stringed pearls or precious stones
Was held by a sealed stone then.

He bore what He bore for us
And stood condemned in our place;
Exalted and generous,
He saved us by love and grace.

Yawakeem ar-Rasi (- 1916).

45 | Tune: Luella, 11s.

Total sovereignty is Yours, O Son of God
Upon Heaven and earth and our earthly clod,
He who trusts You fears not ruin or death's rod
When he enters the dark prison of the tomb.

Chorus
O Christ of God, Mary's son, born of her womb,
You give life to rotten bones held in the tomb.

You killed death when You died on the cross that day,
Frightened the grave when You lodged, but not to stay;
My beloved when loved ones cast me away,
My friend when the nations rise to life or doom.

The dwellers on high, the righteous and the pure
Saw the Holy with men whose sin was mature;
Life of all, the whole of life that will endure,
You tasted death in our place, our dear Bridegroom.

Ibraaheem al-Hoorani (1844-1916).

46 | Tune: Ebenezer, 8,7,8,7,8,7.

Night fell and its curtains scattered
Darkening half of the day
And the dumb hard rocks were shattered
So why did this happen, pray?
Life's Lord, crucified and battered
Tasted death, despised, that day.

See His nailed hands, oh how they bled!
Big nails in the wood did hold;
A crown of thorns sat on His head
Instead of a crown of gold;
Oh, cruel enemies misled
Who worked this in days of old.

Come, hear His agonizing cry
Rising from His broken heart;
See how His blood of darkened dye
Gushed from His side, cleft apart;
Why was this so? Do you know why?
Can you grasp it though in part?

He was a most mighty sovereign,
But He let His glory by
To redeem the sinful whose sin

Angered his Father on high.
And to bring rebellious men in
He came from beyond the sky.

We were born in iniquity
Under wrath to die thereby.
But he redeemed us with pity
From the flames that never die.
Sinners, hear with solemnity
And thus know the reason why.

Lift up your hands pray with true faith,
Thank the Lord of redemption;
Ask forgiveness with all your breath,
Prostrate, call this injunction:
You willingly accepted death
To save us from destruction.

Anonymous.

47 | Tune: Passion Corale, 7,6,7,6,7,6,7,6.

His crown was braided with thorns,
Yes, for my sake indeed,
Causing His noble fair brow
With its dry thorns to bleed;
Guilty hands had placed it there
With ugly scorn driven
When the Saviour's head was crowned,
Righteous Lord of Heaven.

Your strength ebbed slowly away,
On the cross You anguished,
Blood bought our pardon that day
Loved One, as You languished.
Your great pains lessen the loads
With which we have to cope;
Your kind spirit and mercy
Enliven our faint hope.

I pray beneath the cross,
Lord, Kneeling with my bowed head;
My Saviour has redeemed me
When His pure blood was shed.

Jesus led me where the dark
Years of existence run,
Gave me life by the cross till
Eternity was won.

George Khoory (b. 1901).

48 | Tune: Lux Eoi, 8,7,8,7,8,7,8,7.

The host of Heaven descended
At the very break of dawn
To the illustrious who ended
His conquest that early morn;
Hear the angels call with gladness
Tell all, Christ rose from the grave,
As they came with glorious brightness
To the women round the cave.

He arose, that One who carried
Mankind's sin, willed or unwilled,
Who at His death said, unhurried:
What was promised was fulfilled.
His glory shone forth most fully,
Above the void tomb it showed
And the throne's Angel was truly
Servant of that grave abode.

He arose, for He accomplished
Salvation throughout the earth;
Punishment for us abolished,
Let us sing with joyful mirth.

He entered glory victorious
With greatness, beyond man's sight,
Our intercessor is glorious,
Now the universe is bright.

Anonymous.

49 | Tune: Praise my soul, 8,7,8,7,8,7.
Regent Square, 8,7,8,7,8,7.

There was joy and great rejoicing
Shouts of cheer beyond the sky,
The host of the Lord were voicing
A sweet anthem up on high,
Hallelujah, Hallelujah;
Praise Him men and magnify.

The Lord Christ indeed has risen,
The first-born of all the dead,
Come, believers, shout with gladness,
Let His fame be widely spread;
Hallelujah, Hallelujah,
Bless the good Saviour, our head.

Every heart is filled with pleasure,
Victory was on Christ's side
For the Lord has indeed risen
After He willingly died;
Hallelujah, Hallelujah,
He is worthy of our pride.

Preach to all the dead and dwellers
Inside graves of stone or clay,

To await the hope of rising
On the Resurrection Day;
Hallelujah, Hallelujah,
Praise God who forgives today.

He crushed death and saved believers
Who all died at the right time,
Opened Heaven's door for all those
He pitied, guilty of crime;
Hallelujah, Hallelujah,
Pray in faith to the sublime.

He called from despair to glory
Criminals of the worst sort;
We shall rise and live beside Him,
Safe in Heaven, fearing nought;
Hallelujah, Hallelujah,
Always magnify our Lord.

Habeeb Girgis (-).

50 | Tune: Like a sound, 8,7,8,7,8,7,8,7.

At the break of dawn one morning,
On the week's first day, with awe,
Glory's Lord arose adorning
His triumph for evermore,
Destroyed death, its power breaking
As angels moved the great stone
While those guarding fell down quaking
With that brilliant light that shone.

Chorus
You trampled on death, once gory,
O Jesus, the Nazarene,
And the beauty of Your glory
Became manifestly seen.

The first of all the dead who rose,
Giving life through victory;
He truly rose from His repose
After dying on the tree.
Lo, the swords of triumph are drawn
Above the enemies' ground

And the hosts of evil that dawn
Fled wailing from field and mound.

You rose from the house of the dead,
Rock of ages, strong and brave,
Granting eternal life instead
To the sleepers in the grave,
And multitudes returned outright
Witnessing that You arose
While Heaven joined earth to cry out:
He arose, yes, He arose.

And the host of Heaven on high
Met their everlasting Lord
In pure mansions beyond the sky
Singing with the sweetest chord
The glory of hell's destroyer
With pure hymns and great applause,
Saying, O mighty Messiah,
You rose and ruined hell's cause.

Mitri al-Haddad (- 1910).

51 | Tune: Christ the Lord is risen, 7,8,8,8,8,8,8,7.

The Christ is risen today,
The reign of darkness has ended,
Our beloved Lord's reign begun,
Righteousness on man descended,
Victory on the cross was won;
Hallelujah, Hallelujah,
The Christ is risen today.

The Christ is risen today,
For death within that tomb became
Life and blessedness that flourished,
And in our Lord Jesus Christ's name
Hell's foundations were demolished;
Hallelujah, Hallelujah,
The Christ is risen today.

The Christ is risen today,
O Heaven, raise a cheerful cry
And let all space be filled with light;
Let the servants of the most high
Sing of their redemption outright;
Hallelujah, Hallelujah,
The Christ is risen today.

Khaleel Gamal (b. 1915).

52 | Tune: Christ is risen, 6,6,6,4.
Chorus: 6,8,10,8,6,7.

To a dark and dim grave
They carried Christ the brave
While from His side a wave
Of His blood flowed.

Chorus
Death, once vanquished, had fled,
Christ gained victory over hell,
See the bright banners wave above His head
In triumph's procession and swell;
O praise Him, O praise Him,
Hallelujah, He arose.

Tender mother of His,
Why the groaning? Why this?
The light in the grave is
His light that showed.

His death and pain became
The death of sin and shame

And in the dark there came
Hope's star that glowed.

His precious blood, there shed
Purifies hearts once dead,
Saves nations from the dread
Of anguish owed.

Anees al-Maqdisi (1855-1977).

53 | Tune: He is Risen, 11,11,9,11,10,10.

She hurried to the tomb, her Jesus seeking
At the first light of dawn, quietly weeping.
He is not here, no, He is not here,
Your noble Lord arose, Mary from death's throes,
The bright lights were shining by His repose
And the angels calling, Jesus arose.

Oh, what a bright morning, immortal and great
When by His noble death, death died at its gate;
The great One rose, yes, the great One rose,
The power of hell failed to keep His soul nailed
We thank our God and praise, our songs ascend:
The grave is now always life's gate and end.

Anonymous

54 | Tune: Victory, 11s.

What a sublime sight, by greatness attended
That lent gazing eyes longing love, though smarting
When our kind Redeemer and Lord ascended
To glory on the day of His departing.

Chorus
What a sublime sight, by greatness attended
That lent the gazing eyes deep love and longing.

He ascended to wear the crown, His by right,
In the presence of the holy One on high;
He went while their eyes followed Him out of sight
To His high abode beyond the cloudy sky.

And there he sat down at the Father's right hand:
The highest position in Heaven or earth
Where the righteous kneel in worship in that land
With respect and recognition of His worth.

The loyal angels came at His departing
To proclaim the good news with joyous intent,

To comfort His disciples who were hurting
That He will return the same way that He went.

He went to prepare mansions for believers
In glorious homelands beyond high heaven's dome,
So praise him and rejoice, He will receive us
When we meet the Lord in our permanent home.

As'ad ar-Rasi (1858-1915).

55 | Tune: Hollingside, 7s, Double.

The Lord had gone out of sight
To His glorious sublime throne
And rose up above all height
Interceding for His own,
For on earth He adopted
Sinless flesh, that Lamb of fame,
And we, by sin afflicted,
Know He bore our guilt and shame.

He knows our weakness truly,
Our troubles of every name.
The time He spent here duly
Could destroy a human frame,
And He knows how each member
Suffers anguish, pain and dread
For he still does remember
What He carried in our stead.

Man of sorrows, He once knew
Every kind of sore distress
And He gives those who pursue
Blessing and comfort in stress.

Let us lay our sorrows when
With anguish our hearts will beat
On Him, and let them be then
A right footstool for His feet.

Saleem Abdul-Ahad (-1960).

56 | Tune: Miles Lane, C.M., 8,6,8,6.

On the throne of our Redeemer
Rests beauty and wonder
And His head is perfectly crowned
With glory and splendour.

The spring of blessings floods and runs
From the Almighty One;
Amidst the nations' greatest sons
None is His equal, none.

His wisdom shames the wisest sage,
His beauty fills Heaven,
And I intend from age to age
That my praise be given.

In my dark night He is my sun,
Through Him dawn will appear,
The moon to my soul, the bright one
When it is full and clear.

If I possessed one thousand hearts
I give my Lord the lot;
He grants me blessings and imparts
All that he will allot.

Ibraaheem Sarkees (1837-1885).

57 | Tune: Christmas, C.M., 8,6,8,6.

Upon the Saviour's brow there shines
The splendour of beauty
And His head is most aptly crowned
With glorious majesty.

A flood of divine grace is seen
Upon His lucent face;
None like Him in Heaven has been
Nor 'midst the human race.

When He saw man drowning deeply
In destruction's wide sea,
He hurried with grace toward him,
His redeemer to be.

My beloved Saviour became
The ransom for my sin
When He died on the cross to take
My guilt and draw me in.

I thank the source of victory,
The life-giver who gave
Grace to His servant and much more:
Triumph over the grave.

He leads me to glorious mansions
By His most skilful arm
And for my part, I give my heart
And all I have and am.

As'ad ash-Shadoodi (1826-1906).

58 | Tune: Evangelists, 8,8,7,8,8,7.

Christ has gained the kingship truly,
Ascended to the throne duly,
Master of created men.
Kings of earth, humble or stately,
Kiss the Son, exalted greatly,
Worship Him with trembling then.

All the troops of the heights crowding
And heaven's hosts overcrowding,
Hail him and sing forth His praise.
Let the dwellers of every land,
Living, coming, dead beforehand
Submit to His name always.

What high throne, though full of wonder,
Or what king replete with splendour
Attained glories like Jesus?
Let all high men on the planet
Whose glory surpassed all, say it,
I am here to serve Jesus.

Search all ages and all races,
All generations and places
And eternity's programme.

Who like Jesus is most splendid?
Among crowds, alone commended?
Who is as great as the Lamb?

Equal in majesty and might
To His Father, eternal light,
Far above the Cherubim.
Everything is His possession
By the Father's own discretion
Who gave everything to Him.

Sulaiman Doomit (- 1901),

59 | Tune:Syrian Air, 8,7,8,7,8,7,8, 7.
Dich zu Lieben, 8,7,8,7,8,7,8,7.

Rise O Singer and sing the name
Of our Redeemer, our love;
With most melodious tunes proclaim
That signal person above,
That One of a sublime nature
Whose lofty glory is rife,
Creator of all in nature
Whose kindness sustains all life.

With no beginning, eternal,
Was before the mountains were,
Holy, most pure and supernal
With majestic robe, most fair,
Sun of righteousness, of grandeur,
Brilliant planet of the morn,
His is perfection and splendour,
None like Him was ever born.

Conqueror, most mighty, unique,
Called the lion, He alone,
Refuge, Saviour, help of the weak,
Everlasting, living stone,
Root of David, most merciful,

Yet of David'd stock He springs,
Exalted bishop, bountiful,
Light of all created things.

Our righteousness, the infinite,
Excels in kindness, God's Word,
Enriches us, compassionate,
Our gentle Shepherd and Lord.
Praise and magnify Him loudly,
All believers everywhere,
Worship and honour Him proudly,
Bless Him always, anywhere.

Asa'd as-Shadoodi (1826-1906).

60 | Tune: Sidon, 11s.

Should my night descend upon me and I see
The clouds of trouble surrounding my sad breast;
Should afflictions or distress pour down on me,
The beloved's words give me comfort and rest.

I shall come back to you and you shall not be
Orphans after my ascension, drawing nigh,
I shall go, the Comforter shall come from me
As I prepare a wide place for you on high.

I give you my peace, therefore do not despair
Nor fear the rule of the archangel who fell,
Nor let death pluck your assurance, to ensnare,
Be confidant, for I have overcome hell.

I return to gather you that you may share
His glory who has no end or beginning
For truly I say to you, you shall be there
With me for ever when time will stop spinning.

Nofel Istfan (1868-1953).

61 | Tune: Chrome, 11,8,11,8.

O Holy Spirit of the most high God, come,
Source of the light of life, descend,
Come upon us that darkness be overcome
In sinful hearts that You can mend.

Your word, O Lord, causes all blindness to flee
Like the moon that brightens the night;
Your presence, O Lord, is exalted and free,
Pervading all creatures with right.

Your peace, O Lord, is the only peace that owns
Strength to ease consciences that prod;
Your spirit gives life to dead decaying bones
For You are the Almighty God.

Grant us Your peace, guide our ways with compassion
When we cross the river of tears;
Crown us at last with Your final redemption
To dwell in the celestial spheres.

Ibraaheem Sarkees (1837-1885).

62 | Tune: Aletta, 7s. Lyne, 7s.

O Spirit that ever glows,
Be to me my fairest light,
Banish my night till there shows
A morning, radiant and bright.

O Spirit, faithful and true,
Purify my sinful heart,
Help me, my strong joy, renew
Mercy that You can impart.

Spirit of comfort, console
My heart with pity and grace,
Heal my wounds and make me whole,
Remove all troubles I trace.

Holy Spirit of God, make
My heart Your abiding throne,
Let other thrones fall and shake,
The kingship shall be Your own.

Naseef al-Yazigi (1800-1871).

63 | Tune: Windham, L.M., 8s.

Sinner, have you heard it once more?
A soft voice like the morning breeze?
A secret voice knocking the door
Of your mean sinful heart at ease?

It says while pointing to the snares
In destruction's path to eschew,
Beware this world's deceitful love,
Rather love Him who redeemed you.

Do not reject it and be wise:
The voice of the Spirit is this
Warning and asking you to choose
Your portion in eternal bliss.

O heedless one, do not despise
God's Spirit with obstinate strife,
The opportunity may lapse,
Beware while you are in this life.

Then listen to the voice that calls,
Rise up to prayer, for He is nigh
And seek help from creation's Lord
If you intend to dwell on high.

As'ad ash-Shadoodi (1826-1906).

64 | Tune: Ellesdie, 8,7,8,7,, Double.

Give me a heart, both pure and clean,
Gracious Lord whom I pursue;
Unveil my eye till all is seen
With Your guidance, straight and true.
Jesus, hear the cry of the weak,
Aid the frailty on my part
That the sinner may come and seek
Your face with his wounded heart.

Your precious righteousness is pure:
There is none other beside;
Your faithful Spirit, calm and sure,
Only He is our true guide.
My God, be forgiving to me,
Guide me through salvation's ways;
My heart will fill with joy and glee
Through my short remaining days.

Come, all sinners, taste of His ways,
Drink life's water, pure and clear;
Our Saviour is worthy of praise,
Keep His covenant with fear.

Give praise and thanks - lag not behind –
To our everlasting Lord;
Let each heart know and soul and mind
His sincere love shed abroad.

Naseef al-Yazigi (1800-1871).

65 | Tune: David, 8,7,8,7.
Dorrance, 8,7,8,7.

O Spirit, consoling spirit,
Comfort me with joy outright
And flood my heart with divine light
That excels all other light.

My eye has seen great multitudes
Seeking refuge hopefully
Until they found grace from their Lord
And followed Him thankfully.

I am only a weak servant
O Master of utmost might;
Strengthen me and confirm my hope,
Light-giver, give me Your light.

I witness, fearless, openly
That You are the only guide,
Then lead me as long as I live,
Grant a new heart, pure and wide.

Give me a meek, patient spirit
Treading submission's pathway;
Watch over my heart with an eye
Slumber cannot overlay.

Naseef al-Yazigi (1800-1871).

66 | Tune: Gordon, 11s.

O beloved Jesus, my merciful prize,
My life's fence and heart's gate with no compromise,
Receive my prayer, O most generous and wise
For You answer prayers of those who agonize.

Chorus
Help me, Almighty intercessor, arise,
Support the one who stumbles and cannot rise.

I shelter in You and yearn with all my heart
That men may receive of salvation a part:
Slumber lasted long in the land, therefore start
To wake men, and let Heaven's voice energize.

Give life, Lord, to rotten bones, almost consumed,
Leave not one soul to darkness to be entombed;
Keep each heart in the fortress of peace, not gloom:
The peace of Christ's redemption, fraught with surprise.

Grant to the weakling a certainty most strong
Through Your faithful Spirit for whose strength we long
And the mighty guidance of Your Book lifelong
That by shunning sin, true life will be our prize.

Hanna Khabbaz (1871-1955).

67 | Tune: Rosmore, 11s (165).
Warum sind der Thranen, 11s.

O lonesome Sleeper, what does this slumber mean?
Arise and stand for God with your youthful skill;
Discard laziness, the hours have passed and been
And the morning sun is high above the hills.

O Sinner, wake up, arise, for time has passed:
Your sun has reached its setting horizon throne;
Leave the darkness, your shroud is approaching fast,
Answer your Master, knower of the unknown.

O lazy one, hurry up because the day
Is passing from you like lightning in the sky;
The vinedresser is waiting, go not astray,
Redeem the time that will not return, but die.

O idle one, why do you scatter away
What your eternal Master asks while you shirk?
The good Lord of the vine waits for you today,
So rise up instantly and begin to work.

Ibraaheem al-Hoorani (1844-1916).

68 | Tune: Shepherd, 11,9,11,9.

Consoling Spirit, ever gleaming with light,
Descend upon us from Your high throne
And pour upon the conscience a grace with might,
A downpour from Your riches alone.

Kindle a love for our gracious Christ this day
Who died on the cross for us to save
The proud guilty sinner who has gone astray
Held in punishment's prison, a slave.

Increase our faith in the Redeemer of men,
Fill hearts with light brighter than the sun;
Purify them from sin and corruption, then
Erase transgression and guilt, each one.

Come, awaken and warn all who are lukewarm,
Spirit, dwell in their inmost being
And let the Lord's peace in the breasts be the norm,
Like a pure river, overflowing.

Emblaze, O Spirit, in us the fire of life
Till we receive power to endure
And rise toward Christ our God who is the Life
Since prophecy became clear and sure.

Guide all our steps to devotion and good deeds
In the service of our glorious Lord;
Make the word of God the best weapon indeed
For triumph in the war, not the sword.

Saleem Kassab (1842-1907).

69 | Tune: Dominus Regit Me, 8,7,8,7.

We give to God our utmost praise
For His all-embracing grace:
He delivered us from the maze
Of Satan's reign and embrace.

O Father, we approach kneeling,
Hoping on our knees that You
Will aid those who come appealing,
So stretch Your hand to us too.

O Jesus, the Almighty Son,
Refuge of those in despair,
We cry for favour to be done
In this precious hour of prayer.

Spirit of our God, descend here
With great power upon us
And for His sake who loved us, hear
And Lord, look down upon us.

Be kind to us for we draw near
With confidence that is sure
And save us from trouble and fear,
Keep us in Your shade secure.

Sulaiman doomit (- 1901).

70 | Tune: Londonderry Air, 11,10,11,10,11,10,11,12.

Praise the Creator of the worlds out of nought,
Sublime, with excellence and goodness fraught,
Who redeemed the guilty sinful slave and brought
Freedom to him from slavery one day.
What love the Father showed by mighty deeds done
To a world far from His love and undone!
Redeemed it by His only begotten Son
That people may receive eternal life for aye.

The Spirit of God is pure, holy and wise,
Gives life to souls and to bodies likewise,
Guidance to holiness is His enterprise,
The door to pure abodes where men will stay.
Eyes have not seen or minds perceived or declared
The wonder, nor have ears of beings heard
What glory the bountiful Maker prepared
For lost mankind whom He kneaded out of earth's clay.

Yowakeem ar-Rasi (-1916).

71 | Tune: He leadeth me, 8s.

Bestower of the guiding light
With light that is truthful, upright,
Granting the redeemed life and sight
Through our Redeemer's love outright,
Bless those who guide your people, bless
Ad every listener whose heart pines;
Shine on believers You possess
The light of righteousness that shines.

Pour on teachers, full or part-time
Your great instructor Spirit, pour;
Direct their footsteps all the time
In paths of truth from Your great store;
Give all hearers keenness, not ease,
Understanding and a pure heart;
The gifts of believers are these,
Providing glory from the start.

Bless the shepherds who lead them then,
Who guide the flock, keep it and mend;
Give the kingdom of Heaven when
Their speeding years come to an end.

Lord, clothe our lives in every part
With righteousness we cannot buy;
The glory of Heaven does start
Upon the earth before we die.

Anonymous.

72 | Tune: Downs, C.M., 8,6,8,6.

O Lord, giver of strength and might,
Deliverance and aid,
Our safeguard and refuge in blight
And secure fort and shade.

My God, look down, consider, hear
From Your highest Heaven,
Grant to a vine You planted here
Expansion like leaven.

O precious purchase, bought dearly,
Ship of deliverance,
I beg for Your welfare clearly
From God with reverence.

O Church, my love is permanent,
A child's love, strong and free,
Should I forget Your covenant,
My right hand, forget me.

And in my prayers I always seek
Your welfare in duress,
Begging for triumph as I speak
From the source of success.

O Lord, maintain Your well-known pledge
And keep her safe always;
Secure her towers, with peace hedge
Her life throughout her days.

Habeeb Girgis (-).

73 | Tune: St. Stephen's, C.M., 8,6,8,6.

The sign of the cross is in place
On you, beloved child,
That you will follow, soon apace,
The Christ, the crucified.

A sign that you will never toss
Your stand at hardship's door,
But 'midst the valiant of the cross
Hold fast in the great war.

To walk the pathway of the Kind,
Carry the cross, not shun
To do great good for lost mankind
In step with the loved One.

O Bearer of redemption's seal
Pictured on your small brow,
You bear a pledge for ever real,
Its precious crown right now.

Fareed 'Audeh (1908-1982).

74 | Tune: Das Walt Gott Vater, L.M., 8s.

You said, O Lord, when on this earth,
Do let the children come to me,
The kingdom of heaven is for those
Who, like them, have trusted in me.

We bring them now with obedience
To Your command, great as the flood,
That the promise of salvation
Be theirs through Your most precious blood.

When You were baptized, Lord, You did
Baptismal water sanctify;
With this, now sanctify this child,
His guide on whom he can rely.

And after he lives out his days:
The peaceful life You will extend,
He will enter Your glory where
He shall receive a glorious end.

Nofel Istfan (1868-1953).

75 | Tune: Duke Street, L.M., 8s.

Gracious Father, for whom we wait,
Son and Holy Spirit, well known,
Come down with Your glory as great
As Your promise so clearly shown.

Behold, a sinner humbly comes,
Encumbered by life's heavy load,
Wanting to be born, to become
A new child of the living God.

Bless, O Lord, his earnest request
That he seeks here most hopefully;
Increase Your grace that he may find
Delight in life, most joyfully.

Anonymous.

76 | Tune: The Blessed Home, 6s, Double.

O Jesus, Son of man,
Bless our youth to a man
That they may always tread
The right way in Your plan.
Grant them deliverance, come,
From evil's reign and house
Until their lives become
Eternity's storehouse.

They, our aim, our strong rope,
Our joy in life's steep slope,
Lead their steps on the road
To everlasting hope,
If time fails to be bright
And men betray our trust,
In trials they are light
By the grace of the Just.

In our Saviour abide,
Our true friend and our guide,
Our helper in distress,
His light will never hide,

His true gospel will lead
To faith and light within,
His loving heart will speed
To forgive all your sin.

George Khoory (b. 1901).

77 | Tune: Beethoven, 8,7,8,7,8,7,8,7.

My heart loves my great Beloved
Who redeemed me by His cross,
Through whose name I gained salvation
That I should not suffer loss.
Nothing pleases or allures me
Beside His most glorious name;
I accept none other but Him,
My true friend and certain claim.

All the yearning of my poor heart
Is for His person alone;
Nothing surpasses my passion
For His glory and His throne,
For my strength and my life are His,
My Lord possesses them all;
He bought me by His blood saving
The worst sinner of them all.

My intellect is for Jesus,
All I have in life and more,
My love, my peace, my hope in prayer
Are from Him whom I adore.

All my heart I give to Jesus,
My treasure, hope and power,
For my boasting and my buttress
Is my Lord's name, my tower.

Habeeb Girgis (-)

78 | Tune: Saviour, like a Shepherd, 8,7,8,7,4,4,7.

I was in the prison of sin
Slave of Satan, the damned one,
With no hope of my salvation
Until mercy's work was done,
And He bought me
And He bought me
And that with His noble blood.

He paid my debt, not with money,
That great Redeemer, I tell,
But ransomed me with His own blood
From the sore torments of hell,
And He bought me
And He bought
And that with His noble blood.

I do not belong to myself,
There is nothing for me here,
All I have is now the Saviour's
Who saves men and calms their fear,
He redeemed me,
He redeemed me
And that with His noble blood.

My time shall be spent while it lasts
Serving my faithful Saviour
With my body and my spirit
And my mind with endeavour,
He redeemed me,
He redeemed me
And that with His noble blood.

As'ad ash-Shadoodi (1800-1906).

79 | Tune: All Saints, L.M., 8s.

If the righteousness of people
Deserves our thanks for good deeds done
And our hearts are kindled, blazing
From the visit of a loved one.

What greater worthy expression
Of thanks can we give to His name
Who redeemed us, dying for us,
Counted guilty, yet free of blame?

At the time of utmost anguish,
At the time of awesome horror,
His love shunned not crucifixion
To save sinners in that great hour.

What tremendous love He had shown
To ransom His people from loss,
Commanded that they remember
Throughout ages, His bitter cross.

So, how can we not remember
The cross of shame on which He died
That our Beloved may enter
Into our cleansed hearts to abide?

Let our hearts be fully engaged
In His service in every place,
Write nothing above their portals
Save His great name of utmost grace.

Naseef al-Yazigi (1800-1871).

80 | Tune: St. Bernard, C.M., 8,6,8,6.

Come, believers, to His body
While in Christ You abide,
Eat, then drink of the blood that flowed
From His pierced, wounded side.

The Lord who saves, only He is
The Son of the Most High,
He left behind His glorious throne
For us, for us to die.

He made Himself a sacrifice
For our sole redemption,
High priest who vanished the darkness
Of sin and destruction.

The sacrifices of the past,
Given in former years,
Pointed to His most precious blood
His agony and tears.

So, come, believers, approach Him,
His blood calls all, not some,
Take the sign of His testament,
Keep it until He comes.

Saleem Abdul-Ahad (- 1960).

81 | Tune: Avon, C.M., 8,6,8,6.

By the word of the most high One,
With reverence untold,
I now do this remembering
Your death, Jesus, my Lord.

Your body, then broken for me,
Life's food that will endure;
Your noble blood, then shed for me,
Makes sinners clean and pure.

How can I forget that anguish,
So great, O Son of God
When Your sweat trickled while in prayer
Like blood upon the ground?

How can I forget a meek Lamb
Who died to cleanse my guilt?
Bore the shame and pain of the cross
When His pure blood was spilt.

I remember the love You showed
Form me, O loving One;
I remember while I remain
In life till life is done.

And when decay shall wrap my mouth
From praise that it be dumb,
Remember me, Lord of men in
Your eternal kingdom.

As'ad ash-Shadoodi (1826-1906).

82 | Tune: Laban, S.M., 6,6,8,6.

I dedicate myself
To Him who formed all lands,
My body and all things that are
Possessed between my hands.

My Creator, assist
A young evangelist,
Bless my calling by Your Spirit,
The sowing and harvest.

Make my life bright as day
To show evil's dark way,
Call sinners to Him who forgives
All those who went astray.

Mediator, by Your name
The good news I proclaim,
Safeguard Your youthful man and flock,
The able and the lame.

I continue in prayer
To guide the unaware,
So lead my steps, O my Master
In Your service and care.

Milhim Thahabiyyah (-).

83 | Tune: Malvern, L.M., 8s.

Blessed are the people who slept
In our Lord Jesus everywhere,
They are at rest and now are kept
From the dwellings of fear and care.

Their works follow them by God's grace
To homes where gladness holds them fast,
They shine like the planets of space
However long the ages last.

We wander in the dark, our state
Is as strangers with a short lease,
Death has become the open gate
To the house of eternal peace.

Let not your sorrow become then,
Should sadness or disaster come,
Like the sorrow of other men
Who have no hope when they succumb.

When God's own die, young or hoary,
Their death is precious in His eye
And He carries them to glory
To a most guarded place on high.

Habeeb Girgis (-).

84 | Tune: Eventide, 10s. (Abide with me)

We come to place this body in the soil
As his soul went to the Lord after toil;
To Him who saved him and who won the spoil
We now commit the sleeper who believed.

To the night ending for those darkened eyes,
To the morn shining in homelands and skies,
To meet before the Merciful and Wise,
We now commit the sleeper who believed.

To the end of grief and toil fully done,
To the start of joy and glory begun,
To permanent love and peace joined in one,
We now commit the sleeper who believed.

To the return of the Lord in the clouds,
To dead saints resurrected from their shrouds,
To seeing friends and kin amidst the crowds,
We now commit the sleeper who believed.

To the attainment of perfection's aim,
To wearing the crown of beauty and fame
To meeting the Lord of most glorious name,
We now commit the sleeper who believed.

Nofel Istfan (1868-1953).

85 | Tune: 11s. Chorus: 5,11.

For the day of passing I earnestly long,
Enough, O stranger, your absence has been long,
Enough, for my love for that land without cloud
Enables my soul to love wearing the shroud.

Chorus
I have no abode
Here where I journey, a stranger on the road.

My life in this country is spent with concern,
In struggle and sorrow that will not adjourn;
There, in eternity, is goodness and joy,
Peace in the Lord of hosts none can destroy.

My soul, in that fair country, not here below,
You will be in glory with Christ whom you know,
So be pleased to depart to Him and quite soon
To wear a bright garment much brighter than the noon.

O guest, who knows this fleeting life will not mend
In this shady world that is destined to end,
O stranger, then seek to fervently pursue
The journey to a new home prepared for you.

Do not fear the weariness of that hard way,
The wing of the Almighty will shade your day,
Prepare for the time when the journey is sure,
Prepare to wear triumph's garment with the pure.

And when you gain entry, then you will perceive
How that glorious home excels what we conceive
And amidst the thousands you shall wear a crown
And meet with the merciful God of renown.

Yousuf Barakaat (-).

86 | Tune: Darwall's 148th, 12,12,8,8.

Above a spacious sea of glass the nations stand,
A strong army shouting with much joy, loud and grand,
Praising with song the great I Am
The song of Moses and the Lamb.

An army that had fought the wild beguiling beast
And triumphed by the strength of Him born in the East;
Through Him they were victorious then
And that well pleased the host of Heaven.

O Dweller in glory before the birth of time
Your mighty perfect works are wondrous and sublime,
You are a Lord that can forgive
All sins to let the sinner live.

Who does not fear Your name, Almighty Lord of right?
O Vanquisher whose throne is the source of all light?
Your just ways of truth will endure,
Perfect works of perfection, sure.

The angels on high fall down and worship Your name
And the creatures You made worship and do the same,
O holy One, we long and thirst
For You the first of all the first.

Yowakeem ar-Easi (1916-).

87 | Tune: The Better Land, 8,7,8,7,8,7,8,7.

O Pilgrims upon the way, say,
Where are you travelling to?
We speed in the Scriptures toward
Our Redeemer, kind and true,
Over the plains and high mountains
To eternal joys in Heaven,
There in paradise to harvest
Fruits of promises given.

O Pilgrim, what are you hoping
To be given in the bliss?
A most brilliant crown of glory,
From the Saviour's hand it is.
And the white garments that cover
The redeemed saved from the brink
Where the river of the garden
Invites the thirsty to drink.

O Pilgrims travelling, come now,
Join our journey from this day;
Come, O People, you are welcome,
Come with us along the way;

Come with us, you are most welcome,
Hear our Redeemer who said,
People, come quickly and receive
The glory that shall not fade.

Saleem Kassab (1842-1907).

88 | Tune: Amsterdam, 7,6,7,6,7,6,7,6.

Rise, my soul, and seek your part
Of the good God will send,
Escape to your source, your start
From all vain things that end.
Every star will disappear
And the lands will perish;
Seek the glory in that sphere
Where it will not vanish.

The river desires the sea
In its descent and course,
Likewise, suns and flames that be
Will return to their source
And the soul where the Lord found
A home where He can stay
Will always turn its heart round
To seek Him all the way.

Pilgrim, leave your tears and turn
To the place of delight;
The Saviour will soon return
With triumph and great might.

We shall meet Him in the air
With thousands of the pure
And together we shall share
Glories that will endure.

Naseef al-Yazigi (1800-1871).

89 | Tune: O how I love Jesus C.M., 8,6,8.6.
Chorus: 6s.

Lord Jesus, You loved us lifelong
Till death, O tender One,
In weakness You trod down the strong,
His fort was overrun.

Chorus
With His love, most curing,
Flowing love enduring,
Loyal love assuring,
With this, Jesus loved us.

You suffered the horror of death
When nailed upon the cross,
Its waves roared on Your head and breath,
Loved One, You felt them toss.

All that You suffered was in lieu
Of our sins, Lord Jesus
And should we ever forget You
You will not forget us.

You finished Your work and did give
Riches beyond telling
In that great rest where we shall live
In Your glorious dwelling.

Antone Badr (-).

90 | Tune: St. Stephen's, C.M., 8,6,8,6.

If Christ had not loved me, undone
I shall be and wretched;
He saved me that meek slaughtered One
By His own blood deep-red.

If the Merciful had not loved
My soul: died for my guilt,
I would not await bliss above
Nor meet my Lord fulfilled.

Had the Almighty loved me not
And vanquished hell to save,
I would in foul Satan's grip rot,
A sad imprisoned slave.

Had the Forgiving loved me not,
With vile men I conspire,
Remain for ever burning hot,
Punished in lasting fire.

I am thankful while time shall last
Or I remain alive,
To Him who ransomed the outcast
And saved my soul to thrive.

Ibraaheem Sarkees (1837-1885).

91 | Tune: God is Love, L.M., 8s.

God is love, so Heaven and earth
Proclaim His love from far and wide;
My tongue shall sing forth all His worth,
My heart loves to be by His side.

God is love, we, now and always
Live in Him and in Him exist
And to His name multiply praise,
His glorious name that will persist.

God is love, our power and strength
And means of life are favours gained
And water and air and life's length
And light are by His works sustained.

God is love, His blessings a fount
That floods on all men, bright or dim;
By love and grace the nations count
As children who depend on Him.

God is love and exalted high
So blessed be His chastisement;
His love heals those ready to die
Like illness mends through men's treatment.

God is love, so rejoice apace,
His love is lasting, never ends;
We shall not be flung from His face,
But shall receive all that He sends.

God is love for He has redeemed,
By His Son's blood, the sinner's soul;
We shall live for ever esteemed
In bliss, in glory, our true goal.

Ibraaheem Saekees (1837-1885).

92 | Tune: Varina, C.M., 8,6,8,6,8,6,8,6.

My soul, praise the Lord and never
His just judgments forget;
He forgives gross sins and ever
Heals all your sickness yet;
Knows our mould and mineral spar
Before the birth of time
Nor ever forgets that we are
Made from the clay and lime.

Our short days can be regarded
As herbs in earth's rich yield;
We flourish in it unguarded
Like flowers of the field
And when the winds storm upon it
It is lost and routed,
Its place cannot be known one bit
Nor from where it sprouted.

The Lord's mercy flows in life's page
On those who fear His name;
From the beginning of the age
To its end stays the same;

Justice follows those in His care,
The children of His flock
Who keep His covenant, aware
Of His command, their rock.

Naseef al-Yazigi (1800-1871).

93 | Tune: God will take care of you, C.M., 8,6,8,6.
Chorus: 6,8,6,8.

Be not sad or troubled in mind,
Fear not destruction too,
Jesus, the Saviour of mankind
Will never forget you.

Chorus
Lord Jesus, You are mine,
My desire, my life, my release,
My refuge and sunshine,
My Saviour, my joy and my peace.

O Crucified for all my sin,
Wrong deeds and evil will,
I see in Your blood's medicine
The balm of all my ill.

Jesus, You are my hope, my all,
My faith in You shall grow,
I shall not let troubles enthrall
My soul in my sorrow.

'Aql 'Aql (1921-1975)

94 | Tune: Stockwell, 8,7,8,7.

To your beloved Redeemer,
Heavy laden, come across,
Cast your burden on your Saviour
At the stained foot of the cross.

You will see a wholesome fountain
Flow from the side of the Lamb
Who killed death, the child of our sin,
By His pierced side and palm.

Hear the Redeemer now calling
The helpless who lost their peace,
Come to me and then you shall live
And your soul shall be at ease.

Come to me because my advent
Was for sinners born to strife;
I am the true bread of heaven,
I am the water of life.

Bear my yoke upon your shoulders,
I am the good shepherd too,
Do not fear a foe or stranger,
I am a strong fort for you.

Therefore, rise up, O poor prisoner
Held by destruction and jailed,
Ask forgiveness, a gift from Him
Who redeemed you and prevailed.

Do not harden your heart, listen
To your tender Saviour's voice,
Be attentive, approach quickly
Before death comes without choice.

As'ad ar-Rasi (1858-1915).

95 | Tune: Come to the Saviour, 9,6,9,6.
Chorus: 9,9,9,6.

Come promptly to Christ Jesus the Lord,
Burdened, weary and sore,
His kindness will ease the heavy load
Upon the burdened laid.

Chorus
Those who choose Jesus above the rest
As their refuge will find Him their rest,
Will live adorned and joyously by
His righteousness arrayed.

The Lord had said, come, do not delay
And I will give you rest;
Hurry before the end of the day
To His protective shade.

His blood heals sinners and by His side
Lies the pasture of peace
The source of life, overflowing, wide,
Quench your thirst unafraid.

As'ad ash-Shadoodi (1826-1906).

96 | Tune: Park Street, L.M., 8s

Today He calls us, whose great love
Fills aching hearts and makes them whole;
Draw near to him for by His side
Life will fill the languishing soul.

And by His death He gave to us
Life's purchased and costly treasure,
So let us follow Him whose gifts
Bestow riches beyond measure.

Arise and glorify His name,
Singing all tunes with great intent
To Him who has brought us into
The grace of the new covenant.

He calls you, saying, come sinners,
Why do you still wander and roam?
Whoever comes to Him shall be
Received in an eternal home.

'Abdullah Watwaat (-).

97 | Tune: Rhine, C.M., 8,6,8,6.

A noble person stands alone
And knocks upon the door,
So open for Him, fearful one
And fear will be no more.

He now knocks the door of conscience,
Heart and mind to console,
Because He asks for an entrance
To save the captive soul.

So, let our hearts be opened wide
To let the faithful in,
For He, by His own precious blood,
Forgave us every sin.

O holy One and great and bright,
Our darkened souls renew,
Shine down upon us with pure light,
Dispel the night from view.

Ibraaheem Sarkees (1837-1885).

98 | Tune: Adore Te, 11s.

O most Loving who died instead of mankind,
Blot out my sin, worthy pardoner, most kind,
Be my helper, I have stumbled like one blind
In transgressions, my beloved, my Jesus.

My strong fortress and my refuge, I consign
To You my safety that relief will be mine,
Help my weakness, source of hope, and underline
My salvation, my beloved, my Jesus.

You call the guilty heedless sinner to rest
Immortal in the pure mansions of the blest,
However great is the sin of my sad breast,
I come to You, my beloved, my Jesus.

You enliven hope in hearts that seek Your face,
Pardoning them if they repent by Your grace,
You forgive the sins of the guilty and base,
Erase my sin, my beloved , my Jesus.

I wandered in sin's valley, look down on me,
Lead me, guide me and have mercy upon me
And as long as my life shall last I shall be
Offering praises, my beloved, my Jesus.

Most generous who came from highest Heaven,
All praise in my prayers shall always be given;
When the day of my life ends, by death driven,
My soul is Yours, my beloved, my Jesus.

George Ford (1851-1928).

99 | Tune: Call. 11s.

Come on, come on, approach closely, guilty one,
The water of life was poured out for your sake;
There is no price to pay, salvation is done,
Redemption is a free gift for you to take.

Come on hurriedly, why do you not esteem
The love of your gracious Creator and God
And refuse to be washed in the purest stream
That can purify you with that precious blood?

Come on hurriedly and put some endeavour,
His mercy remains calling you while it may,
But in the silent grave its voice will never
Be heard as it leaves you and hurries away.

Come on hurriedly, for the Spirit of grace
If insulted will go far away from you
And your search will end in the darkness you trace
As you descend to eternal darkness too.

Come on, for the time is approaching quite fast
When the earth and the sky will dissolve away
And people will gather to be judged at last,
So, who will save you on the great Judgment Day?

Naseef al-Yazigi (1800-1871).

100 | Tune: Unser Herrscher, 8,7,8,7,8,7.

Come, O Sinners, repent quickly
To the mighty God on high;
Gain the righteousness of Jesus
That hides disgrace, your ally;
Be clothed with Him, be clothed with Him
Before the age passes by.

Come and seek God on this good day
When hope can be known and born,
Before he comes with grave justice
Severe and cannot be borne;
Proceed to Him, proceed to Him
Through the Lamb that once was lorn.

He is merciful and tender,
Pardons sin and is most kind,
Patient, with a heart of pity,
Lover of peace to the mind;
Come and worship, come and worship,
He is the Lord of mankind.

Forsake your deeds of rebellion,
Transgressions in every part;

Accept His consoling Spirit,
Spur that Liar from the start;
You will receive, you will receive
Grace to give life to the heart.

You shall go forth with rejoicing
And with true peace you shall blend;
You will hear a voice of singing
The mountains and hills will send;
Come and seek Him, come and seek Him,
You shall have a pleasant end.

Yousuf Badr (-).

101 | Tune: Greenwood, S.M., 6,6,8,6.

How right that our eyes should
With hidden water flow
When the tender Lord of Heaven
Wept for the sinner's woe.

The angels saw God's Son
Weeping sinners condemned
And were amazed to see His tears
Flow for their wretched end.

Jesus the Saviour wept
That you may find true peace,
O Soul imprisoned, shed your tears
For healing and release.

He wept that we may weep
For sinners lost, forlorn;
There is no weeping in Heaven,
But joy no man has known.

As'ad ash-Shadoodi (1826-1906).

102 | Tune: St. Columba, C.M., 8,6,8,6.

My soul will be at peace if I
Live for the Crucified
Who washes sin of deepest dye
Since for my sake He died.

Jesus, whose saving work was done
Through a torrent of blood,
Wash and cleanse me, a guilty one,
By that most noble blood.

Master, listen to my request
And show love on Your part;
Accept a sinner whose behest
Is a repentant heart.

Let my heart feel within my breast
Your mercy and Your grace;
My hope in You alone will rest,
Hide my sins without trace.

Milhim Thahabiyyah (-).

103 | Tune: Madrid, 7s.

O Jesus, my rock and bliss,
I find my rest in Your shade;
In hunger and nakedness
I, a sinner, seek Your aid.
My soul has nothing to bring
That can count worthy and meet,
But with grievous wounds that sting
Your servant stands at Your feet.

Satisfy me each moment
With mercy that dispels fear
And clothe me with a garment
And make my mind pure and clear.
Trouble fills me and illness
O Physician, as You see,
Heal my soul in its weakness,
Bestow Your peace and save me.

My portion in every part
And tender Redeemer too,
You can comfort my sad heart
When death comes to grin and woo.

My precious Deliverer
Who is in glory on high,
Be my fort, my rescuer
And my rich crown when I die.

Saleem Kassab (1842-1907).

104 | Tune: Aberystwyth, 7s Double.

From most trustworthy Jesus
I seek safety and shelter
As the winds, strong and parlous
Submerge me in deep water.
Grant me a sure hiding-place,
Guide me to secure port
And when death shows its mean face,
Let a peaceful end be wrought.

My helper, in You I stand,
Rely on You, to You flee,
Cover my head with Your hand
Like a strong wing shading me.
My sufficiency and need,
I desire You all the time,
My love for You shall indeed
Be unlimited, sublime.

Raise the fallen and the weak,
Encourage Your servant's mind;
Heal the seek and those who seek
Your leading when lost and blind.
You are holy and upright,
Lord of truth, blessing and grace;

I, a sinful slave whose plight
Is deeds, both futile and base.

O merciful God and just,
Tender and forgiving sin,
Cleanse me within from all lust
And keep me outwardly clean.
You, the spring of life and peace,
I have drunk, but I need more;
Flood my heart and still increase,
Flood it now and evermore.

Naseef al-Yazigi (1800-1871).

105 | Tune: Gethsemane, 7s.

O beloved Friend of mine,
Hope of sinners everywhere,
Helper and hearer, divine,
Accept and answer my prayer,
A lowly spirit endow
My beloved Jesus, now.

I was born of sinful seed
Amidst enemies of right,
Have nothing, but faults indeed,
Wounds and sore sickness that blight;
I am saved if now I cling
To Jesus, my Saviour King.

I have no friend, only You
O Lord Jesus, ever blest
And when You are in my view
Then my soul abides at rest
And to You I humbly bow
O my Hope, my Jesus, now.

So, accept my thankfulness,
The praise of joy I bring in

And my hymns of happiness,
O Lord who forgives my sin
And when sleep becomes too strong,
Take my soul, Jesus, my song.

Sulaiman Doomit (1901-).

106 | Tune: Mendebras, 7,6,7,6,7,6,7,6.

Who helps the held and weary
In grief, sorrow and ill?
In frightening states, most eerie
With hope crushed in the mill?
I called, Lord, I am dreary,
My load troubles me still;
Give faith that does not query,
Remove my chains with skill.

O Goal of my hope and need,
Desire of heart and sight,
My works have floundered indeed
And held me in my plight.
Pity my poor state with speed,
My hour of dismal fright
And let my burdens recede
O Root of love and light.

He stretched to me His right hand
With help that was made clear;
His bowels pitied a strand
With compassion, so dear,
Placed me in His care to stand,
Secure and without fear

And His favours still surround
My soul with kindness here.

He smiled and said, be at ease,
I am your Shepherd now,
My protection will not cease,
My strength will shield Your brow,
Evil shall not steal Your peace,
No harm will I allow,
Trust my words while I increase
Blessings, and grace endow.

As'ad ar-Rasi (1858-1915).

107 | Tune: Old 22ND D.C.M., 8,6,8,6,8,6,8,6.

I cannot proceed on the way
O most merciful One,
Pity a prisoner, astray,
Sinful, guilty, undone.
Your blood provides my salvation,
Redeemer of great might,
Be my hope and consolation
And my sure guiding light.

Have mercy, my strength is feeble,
Master, kind and grand;
No helper steadies my wobble
Or strengthens me to stand.
O Spring of wisdom, pure and keen,
Be my support, I pray,
Perfection of Your strength is seen
When weakness plagues my way.

Blind in this world, none to guide me,
Yes, none to be my eyes,
Lead my steps and walk before me
To Your dwelling on high.

My strength has flagged, I may some day
Hear clearly, not amiss,
The Merciful say, come away,
Enter into the bliss.

Asma Ra'd (1888-1978).

108 | Tune: Beecher, 8,7,8,7, Double.

If calamities assail me
And companions stay away,
If disasters will surround me
And friends disappear for aye,
Then the Lord Jesus, my bright light
Will shine in my darkest day,
My peace and sun in my black night,
My portion and joy and stay.

If I reap after endeavour
Disappointment, shattered hope,
Or expect goodness for ever
And in failure left to grope,
Then my faith brings consolation
Despite trial and falsehood,
For all things in this salvation
Work for the believer's good.

If I harvest from a loved one
Bitter fruits of anguished grief,
If I see vanity outrun
All things here, without relief,
Then my Lord Jesus, my treasure
Will stay with me everywhere

And His armies do His pleasure
In my service and my care.

When my longing soul is eager
To enter my heavenly rest,
Jesus' name, my intercessor
Lets me in with all the blest
Where His glory shines for ever
As I look upon His face
Where eternal blessings cover
All His people saved by grace.

Sulaiman Doomit (1901-).

109 | Tune: Rouen Church Melody, 7s.

Lord, You are my peace and ark,
My purpose, my aim and mark,
I shall walk in Your bright light
That makes sunshine of the dark
And after death lights its spark,
I rise to Your highest height.

Hurriedly, I came to You,
Casting my burdens on You,
Asking for comforts unpriced,
Seeking favours I pursue
While my trust has hitherto
Been in You, my Saviour Christ.

Be to my soul a support,
To my thought, guidance unbought,
My wish shall be Your pleasure.
Let my weaknesses abort
And at ruin I shall snort
Safe in You without measure.

George Khoory (1879-1968).

110 | Tune: Arms of Jesus, 7,6,7,6,7,6,7,6.

My soul in the arms of Jesus
Is securely at rest,
Surrounded by His great love
In His most spacious breast.
Above the water, listening,
Above the green meadow,
I hear the angels singing,
Moving like a shadow.

Chorus
My soul in the arms of Jesus
Is securely at rest,
Surrounded by His grat love
In His most spacious breast.

If my sorrow lasted long
And my suffering was great,
Most of it has passed along:
Days of trial abate.
If my sins rage to fulfill
My ruin and demise,
The knower of secrets will
Free me and stabilize.

Jesus shelters and sustains
My soul: He died for me,
Rock of ages that remains
Lord of good pledged for me.
I await patiently still
The shining of that light
On that famous morn that will
Expel my bitter night.

Sarah Sabra (1849-1915).

111 | Tune: Love Divine, 8,7,8,7,8,7,8,7.

O Lord Christ, be to me indeed
A buttress each passing hour,
Make my works like righteous men's deeds,
More worthy by Your power,
You love filling my heart fully,
It loves none other but You,
I beg closeness to You truly,
Loving You and pleasing You.

Lord, my proud aim without measure
Midst my people in the land,
And, Master, You are my treasure,
In my grief a helping hand.
Restorer of the dead to life,
You made the blind man to see,
Helped the burdened with guilt and strife,
Took his load and made him free.

Likewise, the leper found healing
In an instant by Your might
And the lame man got up feeling
That his legs held him upright.

We believe in You, our keeper
Who protects us from all ill
And out thanks shall be much deeper
O Saviour of mankind still.

Yousuf al-Aseer (1814-1889).

112 | Tune Londonderry Air, 11,10,11,10,11,10,11,12.

O my God and Master, pity my sad plight,
I roamed in deserts of what is not right;
My foe set for me snares of evil and blight,
Armies of ruin to grind me and sieve.
Have compassion, Master, pity my weakness,
Bind my deep wounds with kindness and meekness,
Heal, my Lord, an ailing soul full of bleakness,
Complaining of dire helplessness, most aggressive.

I cry to You in my despair and sorrow,
Pardon my sins today, not tomorrow,
Sanction release to my soul, heart and marrow,
Pity the guilty and lost and forgive.
Jesus, Nazarene, friendly and supportive
Halt my transgressions from being active,
Help the wretched culprit, now a fugitive
Who cries to the Lord: have mercy, be receptive.

I gave myself to the Crucified to bear,
My grief, to break the shackles of despair.
Should I sleep one day, the pledge of my grave's share,
My pledgee commands the entombed to live.

Therefore, to that day my soul has longed and yearned,
My wounds healed at His bidding, health returned.
Hurry up, my King, my Christ, for I have learned
To make Your craved-for coming my firm objective.

As'ad ar-Rasi (1858-1915).

113 | Tune: Bread of Heaven, 7s.
Pilot: 7s.

Guide my soul, O Jesus Lord,
As I tread this vale of tears,
In life's troubles and bleak road
Be salvation's rock from fears.
You, my guide, are my reward,
Guide my soul, O Jesus, Lord.

Yours the glory and great might,
Stilling the waves of the sea;
Tempests, storms, submit in flight,
Earth and sky at Your decree.
Saviour of an endless horde,
Guide my soul, O Jesus, Lord.

When the final hour has run
And I see the peaceful shore,
Welcome me, beloved One
And receive me evermore
And in homelands, fair and broad,
Guide my soul, O Jesus, Lord.

Ibraheem Sarkees (1837-1885)

114 | Tune: Ministres de l'Eternal, 7s.

Planet of the morning, glow
From behind the darkest night;
Flood life with Your brilliant light,
Guide us wherever we go;
The source of the light and hope,
Refresh our souls lest we grope.

Be to all believers, be
Wherever they walk, a friend;
Guard them in straits and defend
And their faithful Shepherd be;
They shall find rest on the way
And under Your shadow stay.

Who have they when trouble brings
In the hour of fear, distress,
With no helper or buttress,
But You, O Lord of all things?
You are a castle of strength
To the world, its breadth and length.

With Your countenance, release
Your sons and let their night cease

And then bring them back in peace,
Glorious after their decease.
O Light of existence, stay
Man's path to an endless day.

Anees al-Maqdisi (1885-1977).

115 | Tune: Chrysostom, 8s.

Yearned-for Spirit of life, our rock,
We, in the midst of darkness, knock
As we wander needing a guide
At hope's portals, crying, unlock.
Grant the visible light that we
The face of the high One may see.

Exterminate the doubts wrapping
These faint hearts and still are sapping
Their strength, and uncover clearly
The sum of what life is mapping.
Grant the visible light that we
The face of the high One may see.

We toiled with other agenda
And went far from our defender
Till the billows covered our heads
And obscured from us Your splendour.
Grant the visible light that we
The face of the high One may see.

Shine on mankind with a bright sheen
Like fair sunlight over the green;

Dispel the darkness all around
That we may see what is not seen.
Grant the visible light that we
The face of the high One may see.

Anees al-Maqdisi (1885-1977).

116 | Tune: Silscher, 7,4,7,4,7,4,7,4.

Take me by the hand, lead me
As You find best
Till I see in my dark night
Heaven's bright rest.
Lord Jesus, walk before me,
Showing the way;
Where You go I shall follow
And ever stay.

Strengthen me in my weakness
By Your mercy
Until I find rest in Your
Sufficiency.
All my trust is in You, Lord,
In grace I stand,
I shall retire safe and whole
Under Your hand.

Wherever my path shall lead
Through a dark bend
My good Lord shall grant to me
A pleasant end.

Take me by the hand and lead me,
Never amiss
Till around me glows and shines
The light of bliss.

Sulaiman Doomit (-1901).

117 | Tune: Nun Kemm der-Heiden, 7s. Heiland, 7s.

O brilliant and splendid Light,
Word of God, mighty and strong,
My soul is eager for flight
To Your side, for whom I long.

My Redeemer, Christ, You are
Lord of all beings alive,
Merit praise from near and far,
Life of all the saints that thrive.

Lord, for how long shall we be
In this world of sore distress?
Young and old we seem to be
Roaming in the wilderness.

Jesus, we long for the state
Of bliss in our home on high
And however long we wait
Our yearning shall never die.

Anonymous.

118 | Tune: Cross of Jesus, 8,7,8,7.

Behold the Lord Jesus had said,
I am the light of the world,
No friend of mine shall be misled
When the guiding truth is heard.

Grant us, our God, a guiding light
In the darkness of this life
To give our souls that pure delight
With joy and peace that are rife.

Lord Jesus, realize to me
The promises of Your word;
By the Spirit, remove from me
Clouds of doubt with worry shared.

When You illumine the dark soul
It promptly reflects Your light,
Like the sun's rays, lent to extol
The moon that brightens the night.

Support the reign of truth's brilliance
In our region where it stands;
Dispel the night of ignorance
O Lord Jesus, from our lands.

Your fair sun has shone upon us
Without setting or decline;
Hurry, Master, come back to us
Upon the bright clouds that shine.

Saleem Kassab (1842-1907).

119 | Tune: Faithful Guide, 7s. Jesus, mein Zuversicht, 7s.

O King of the world, and head
Of believers widely spread,
Rule my heart that it be led
By Your faithful Spirit, shed;
Possess me, my help in dread
O King of the world and head.

Sovereign of the ages, pure,
Evil's conquest did procure,
Grant me strength that will endure,
Be my walled fortress, secure
From deception's snares that lure,
Sovereign of the ages, pure.

Master, hearer of my prayer
From Your high exalted chair,
Let obedience be my share
O Saviour, gentle and fair;
Mediator, grant help and care,
Master, hearer of my prayer.

George Ford (1851-1928).

120 | Tune: Abends, L.M., 8s.

A precious name, sublime, ever
Above every exalted name,
Jesus, Saviour and life-giver
To worn out souls He came to claim.

Who amongst men of all ages
Can stubbornly reject His love?
Or make light of or despise
His Crucifixion and death thereof?

The Father's favour rests on us
For His Son's sake, for His alone
And the Spirit, with them One, thus
Assists us when we pray and groan.

When Christ's face shall at last appear
My hope will mix with joy that day;
His name removes all dread and fear,
His presence casts evil away.

Naseef al-Yazigi (1800-1871).

121 | Tune: Gerontius, C.M., 8,6,8,6.

I offer You, O Lord on high
My everlasting praise
For Christ's redemption when I was
Lost in my sinful ways.

It was He, with wondrous kindness
And love, with self denied,
Who gave Himself freely for us
When on the cross He died.

And You gave Your Holy Spirit
O Son of God, to us
And thus the grave became the door
Of life and happiness.

Holy, holy, is God the Lord,
Most holy is our God,
None is ever like Him abroad
And He remains our God.

Najeeb Mash'alaani (-).

122 | Tune: Gethsemane, 7s.

O forgiving Redeemer,
Rock of ages, my shelter,
Wipe out sin, O Merciful,
Help the guilty and shameful,
Purify me with Your blood
Hearer of my prayer, my God.

You forgive iniquity
And cover wrongs with pity
And guide those who go astray,
Therefore, guide my soul today;
I shall live for You alone,
Pure like angels round Your throne.

When the time will come at last
And all work rests in the past,
Take me home, my guardian guide
Where I shall be by Your side,
O forgiving Redeemer,
Rock of ages, my shelter.

As'ad ash-Shadoodi (1826-1906).

123 | Tune: All to Christ I owe, 6s. Moseley, 6s without chorus.

Come to the Redeemer,
O weak one, sore and blind,
He who is Almighty
Will help, for He is kind.

Chorus
The Redeemer of man
Wipes out, sins for He can,
Making their crimson stain
Like snow on hill and plain.

The blood of the Saviour
Washes away all sin
And His Holy Spirit
Purifies hearts within.

He who died for my guilt,
His cross is my sure pride,
I have no righteousness
But His who bled and died.

I shall meet Him when He
Returns back from Heaven
And rise up toward Him
In the air, forgiven.

In His highest glory
I shall ever remain
For by His precious blood
He cleansed me from all stain.

As'ad ash-Shadoodi (1826-1906).

124 | Tune: Dennis, S.M., 6,6,8,6.

If my soul, stained with sin
Like crimson, it will seek
To be whiter than the snow in
Lebanon's mountain peak.

In dire straits or in pain
And when my grief is full,
I fear no evil, but will gain
Help from the Merciful.

If my foes assault me
With the armies of hell,
No one shall ever enthral me:
My Saviour saves me well.

The shield of faith is mine
And the Spirit's sharp sword
And hope's helmet, with help divine,
Will give me my reward.

Ibraheem Sarkees (1837-1885).

125 | Tune: Rathbun, 8,7,8,7.

If we sailed the waves of the sea
Calmly to our hoped-for rest,
If the wind helped us, it would be
Of God's goodness who knows best.

If it raged, tossed us to and fro,
Sank us in the wet azure,
It would speed our short journey to
The fair homeland of the pure.

Grant us, Lord, obedience to do
What is Your wish and desire;
In supreme joy and sorrow too,
Hear us and answer our prayer.

Bid Your spirit of comfort hence,
Who made our hearts His abode,
To console us if our patience
Perished along our set road.

The Lord quickly rescues His own
In their trouble and sore stress;
Their faithful companion, well known
As their best friend in distress.

Ibraheem al-Hoorani (1844-1916).

126 | Tune: St. Clement, 9,8,9,8.

O Guardian of the vast universe,
I surrender myself to You,
Disregard me not, nor disavow
For I have placed my trust in You.

Watch over me lest I go astray
And deliver me from my foe,
Guide me and lead me in every way
Till in Redemption's path I go.

When the darkness comes to surround me
With worry spoiling my life's day,
Let me glimpse Your smile and let it be
The chaser of sorrow away.

When illness plagues me until I see
My sun set at its journey's end
And mankind becomes distant from me,
Then, Beloved, be my close friend.

Rizq al-Haddad (- 1945).

127 | Tune: Duane Street, L.M., 8s.

If I walk in the wilderness
He is at my right and left hand,
Jesus, Lord of triumph, no less,
I trust in Him and in Him stand.
Jesus, my pattern at whose cost
My soul strives in this wretched world:
He drew me when I wandered, lost,
Banished darkness and light unfurled.

I am what I am and shall be
Only by God's goodness and grace;
His blessings flow and surround me
In every state of life and place.
Lord, turn my eyes that they may see
That most noble and precious blood,
See me always and look on me
Through His face, my Redeemer God.

Your love, my Master, has broken
The gates of hell and Satan's might;
By Your eternal love's token
I gain my home of bliss and light.

Your Spirit in me will bestow
All strength with happiness and peace,
By Him, most high, I live and grow
Through Your blessings that never cease.

Ibraheem Sarkees (1837-1885).

128 | Tune: Lyndhurst, 11s.

My heart's hope and my life's light, whom I adore,
O lovely Jesus, Lord of peace, without guile,
Heal my soul and guide me to salvation's door
And turn toward me with kindness and a smile.

My sins have embittered my soul and laid me
In the oceans of despair and dreadful fear,
Pluck me out and remove disasters from me,
Have pity and mercy, O Shepherd, most dear.

My Salvation, I have no shield beside You
From death's darts, O Reviver of souls alone,
When, oh when, my Master will my eyes see You
On Your seat of glory and majestic throne?

Light of the universe and Heaven's bright light
O Christ of God, believers' Saviour and King,
Shine on my heart, scatter the clouds of night
That I may see Your love like the clear morning.

I submitted my heart to Your holy hands
O Peace to my heart when awful fear is nigh,
Can I dread death when he who enters that land
Rests in that majestic fair abode on high?

My portion on the day when the graves shall break
When You return in the clouds, my joy and stay,
Remember, forgive Your servant when I wake
In hope on the Day of Reckoning, that day.

As'ad ar-Rasi (1858-1915).

129 | Tune: Colyton, 11s.

When the darkness enshrouds my soul for a while
And in the grip of horrible night I toss,
I watch the dawn, while on my face a smile
As I observe it rising above the cross.

And if the sun has gathered its shining gold
From the edge of the horizon of fair wings,
Then my soul will humbly converse with its Lord
And see in the night, secrets the morning brings.

I fear not the terror of death or sorrow
While my heart keeps of hope a firebrand or ray,
You shall be leaving today or tomorrow
So make the provision for that eternal day.

However the waters of the pure brook flows
To the sea, singing, murmuring in motion,
Likewise my soul yearns for the most high it knows,
Eagerly waiting to join the deep ocean.

Wadee' Deeb (b.1891).

130 | Tune: Something for Jesus, 6,4,6,4,6,10.

Increase Your love to me
My loving Friend
And answer my prayer when
I kneel and bend.
My desire is no less
Than of love an excess
An excess of love for the Redeemer.

I aimed with emphasis
To attain bliss
And now in my good Lord
I find this.
My great wish, I profess
Is of love an excess,
An excess of love for the Redeemer.

I do not dread sadness,
Bane or hardness,
For this will pour on me
Blessed gladness,
Then my heart will possess
Of love a great excess,
An excess of love for the Redeemer.

When time comes for the door
Of life to slam,
Then, O my Soul, repeat
Praise to the Lamb.
You will see and confess
The Lord of love, no less,
The Lord of love no less: the Redeemer.

Nqoola Nimr (-).

131 | Tune: Das Walt' Gott Vater, L.M., 8s.

I have obtained peace from my Lord
And this is sufficient for me,
He took my heart's fear and discord
And victory comes from Him to me.

But should great distress interpose,
My tongue will then set forth its cause;
My God will grant my heart repose
And fair patience will endow me.

His cross cancelled my guilt and sin,
His ransom gave me life within,
He is the refuge I hide in,
His love is now a faith to me.

He rewards me when I repent
And makes my ways happy, well-spent;
Should I die for my faith unbent,
He gives life after death to me.

There shall be no peril to bear,
The garden of the just is there
And then my choice Master, most fair,
In His eternal home keeps me.

Fareed 'Audeh (1908-1982).

132 | Tune: Angers Church Melody, D.C.M., 8,6,8,6,8,6,8,6.

I love the Lord, but not to gain
An everlasting bliss
Nor to be saved from the torment
Of hell and the abyss,
But I love Him because His love
Is sweet to me and more;
It was He by His good pleasure
Who loved me long before.

He, only He, was for our sakes
Insulted like a slave
And bore the suffering of the cross
And the sleep in the grave,
And though, rich, yet in our world lived
With poverty His share
And that for His enemies' sake,
Where is His equal, where?

Far be it that I should worship
Him who lifted my load
For greed of Heaven or for fear
Of hellfire's grim abode;

Not so, but only that my Lord
Had loved me for His part
And for His sublime attributes
I love Him with my heart.

As'ad ash-Shadoodi (1862-1906).Based upon - My God I love Thee - by Francis Xavier (1506-1552) and translated into English by Edward Caswall
(1814-1878).

133 | Tune: Meribah, 8.8.6, Double.
Ariel, 8,8,6, Double.

If in the Saviour you grow old
Die in His love, intense and bold,
Thanking that glorious friend,
You have not perceived one atom
Nor measured one drop to fathom
Profuse love without end.

Death and hell dread His glorious might;
He dashed His opponent outright,
The foe's power and sway.
The planets of morning desired
To reach Him, but never acquired
Guidance on any day.

Lo!, none but God knows fully well
Or fathoms perfectly to tell
The secret of His love.
May the thirsty heart in the land
Of drought find sure relief at hand
By means of his Lord's love.

I trust, at last, I shall be meet
To be before my loved One's feet

In that highest station;
Beside Him, what joy I shall raise!
His love the start of all my praise,
The joy of salvation.

Moosa al-Khoory (-).

134 | Tune: Lower lights, 8,7,8,7.

Rise, believers, fight corruption,
The host of haters of right;
The world's Saviour gave instruction
To withstand the wrong and fight.

Chorus
Sing melodious hymns most proudly
Of Christ's conquests and Christ's ways
And raise up your voices loudly
With countless songs in His praise.

Arise, witness to His lordship,
Carry light's banner unfurled
And spread the spirit of worship
Reverently in this world.

The world shall give you much hardship,
Just as God's true Book had said,
But the great Redeemer's friendship
Will be your reward instead.

Your call to us, Lord, was concrete,
To gain souls, lost and misled;
Strengthen us and entrench our feet
In the holy path we tread.

Khaleel Assaf Bisharah (1876-1950).

135 | Tune: Hold the Fort, 8,5,8,5.

The soul's enemy draws his sword,
Dauntless, of great might,
Roars like a lion in the sward,
Requesting a fight.

Chorus
Lo! Christ the Lord is approaching,
Fortify the forts,
Fear not a tyrant encroaching,
A traitor that snorts.

The enemies of right are like
Lions in the field,
So rise, soldiers, prepare to strike
With weapons and shield.

Raise the banner of faith today,
The troop's shout is high,
The sword of truth gleams in the fray,
Victory is nigh.

Our great war is fire that feeds
Like a mighty flame,
Our loving Redeemer who leads
Is of glorious fame.

The grace of our great Lord is sweet,
Helps us to endure;
How can we dread any defeat?
Our triumph is sure.

Saleem Kassab (1842-1907).

136 | Tune: Fount, 8,7,8,7,8,7,8,7.

Blind son of Timaeus cried out:
Jesus, pity Your young man;
Others received healing from You,
Help my frailty, for You can.
The crowd angrily rebuked him,
He cried louder, paid no heed;
The Lord called him: come now to me
And then ask me what you need.

He did not want goods that perish
Despite his impoverished state,
But he sought for the Lord's mercy,
Only He could allocate.
He said, I beg light for my eyes
You can give that they may see;
His eyes were then opened outright,
He followed Him thankfully.

Hear him calling with great fervour
And with joyful songs of praise;
Look friends, the glorious Redeemer,
Mercy shows in all His ways;

May all the blind know the healer,
Only He can heal the blind
And give to His faithful followers
New sight for the eye and mind.

Naseef al-Yazigi (1800-1871).

137 | Tune, Long, long ago, 10,8,10,7,10,10,7

Jesus my Lord approaches sinner with love
Long, long ago, long, long ago,
For their sakes He left His fair home above
Long, long ago, long ago,
For them He tasted the death of the cross,
Who like this loved One can leave all for dross?
But this hides the greatest wonder, not loss
Long, long ago, long ago.

What lover would be devoted and free
Long, long ago, long, long ago?
To die for hated men like you and me
Long, long ago, long ago?
But Christ who saved us from our race when we
Were far away, oblivious and carefree,
His love, redeemed us from doom, on the tree
Long, long ago, long ago.

His loving kindness had covered our head
Long, long ago, long, long ago,
He chose to ransom our race, once misled,
Long, long ago, long ago.

He did not keep those before us who spread
Into the world and made evil their bread,
But the Lord destroyed the earth with much dread
Long, long ago, long ago.

As'ad ash-Shadoodi (1826-1906).

138 | Tune: O Galilee! L.M., 8s.

I was chained by iniquity
And justice proclaimed my demise;
The Lord paid my indemnity,
Loosed and saved me and said, arise.

Chorus
My Saviour died on Calvary
To grant me favour and erase
My sins upon that cruel tree,
Beloved, I shall sing Your praise.

He did not leave His awesome throne,
Forsaking His riches on high,
But to release prisoners forlorn
Till for His grace they thirst and cry.

My spirit, my body and strength
Are His who saved me by His blood;
I live to please Him through life's length,
My joy the favour of my God.

I always thank my living Head,
Father and Spirit, all divine,
And Son whose precious blood was shed
That everlasting peace be mine.

Dawood Qurban (1860-1935).

TUNES

Tune: Trinity, 6 & 4s . (Thou whose almighty word)

Tune: Old Hundredth, L.M. 8s. (All people that on earth do dwell)

Tune: St. Albans. 11s. (Immortal, invisible)

Tune: Melita, L.M., 8s. (Eternal Father, strong to save)

Truro, 5 verses, no chorus. (Jesus shall reign where'er the sun)

Tune: St. George's, Windsor, 7s,D. (Christ the Lord is risen today).

Tune: Hamburg, L.M., 8s (O God, before whose alter)

Tune: Rest, L.M., 8s (The saints of God, their conflict past)

Tune: Helmsley, 8,7,8,7,4,7. (Lo, he comes with clouds descending)

Tune: Marching, 8,7,8,7. (Father, hear the prayer we offer)

Tune: Abridge, C.M., 8,6,8,6. (Be thou my guardian and my guide)

Tune: Lahee (Nativity), C.M., 8,6,8,6. (Come, let us join our cheerful songs)

Tune: Herald Angels, 8,7,8,7,8,7,8,7. (Hark the herald angels sing)

Tune: Dix, 7s. (As with gladness men of old) Melita, 8s. (Eternal Father, strong to save)

Tune: Angelus, L.M., 8s. (At even, ere the sun was set)

Tune: Passion Corale, 7,6,7,6,7,6,7,6. (O Sacred head, once wounded)

Tune: Lux Eoi, 8,7,8,7,8,7,8,7. (Alleluia, alleluiah, Hearts to Heaven..)

Tune: Praise my soul, 8,7,8,7,8,7. (Praise, my soul, the king of heaven)

Tune: Hollingside, 7s, Double. (Jesu, lover of my soul)

Tune: Miles Lane, C.M., 8,6,8,6. (All hail the power of Jesus' name)

Tune: Evangelists, 8,8,7,8,8,7. (Come, pure hearts in sweetest measure)

Tune: Dominus Regit Me, 8,7,8,7. (The King of love my Shepherd is)

Tune: Saviour, like a Shepherd, 8,7,8,7,4,4,7. (Saviour, like a shepherd lead us)

Tune: Darwall's 148th, 12,12,8,8. (Ye holy angels bright)

Tune: Love Divine, 8,7,8,7,8,7,8,7. (Love divine, all loves excelling)

Tune: Bread of Heaven, 7s. (Bread of Heaven, on thee we feed)

Tune: Chrysostom, 8s. (Jesu, my Lord, my God, my all)

Tune: Cross of Jesus, 8,7,8,7. (Come, thou long-expected Jesus)

Tune: Abends, L.M., 8s. Glory to thee, my God, this night)

Tune: Gerontius, C.M., 8,6,8,6. (Praise to the Holiest in the height)

Tune: St. Clement, 9,8,9,8. (The day Thou gavest, Lord, is ended)

Tune: O Galilee! L.M., 8s. (Jesus shall reign where'er the sun)

Tune: Trinity, 6 & 4s . (Thou whose almighty word)

Tune: Old Hundredth, L.M. 8s. (All people that on earth do dwell)

Tune: St. Albans. 11s. (Immortal, invisible)

Tune: Melita, L.M., 8s. (Eternal Father, strong to save)

Truro, 5 verses, no chorus. (Jesus shall reign where'er the sun)

Tune: St. George's, Windsor, 7s,D. (Christ the Lord is risen today).

Tune: Hamburg, L.M., 8s (O God, before whose alter)

Tune: Rest, L.M., 8s (The saints of God, their con[lict past)

Tune: Helmsley, 8,7,8,7,4,7. (Lo, he comes with clouds descending)

Tune: Marching, 8,7,8,7. (Father, hear the prayer we offer)

Tune: Abridge, C.M., 8,6,8,6. (Be thou my guardian and my guide)

Tune: Lahee (Nativity), C.M., 8,6,8,6. (Come, let us join our cheerful songs)

Tune: Herald Angels, 8,7,8,7,8,7,8,7. (Hark the herald angels sing)

Tune: Dix, 7s. (As with gladness men of old) Melita, 8s. (Eternal Father, strong to save)

Tune: Angelus, L.M., 8s. (At even, ere the sun was set)

Tune: Passion Corale, 7,6,7,6,7,6,7,6. (O Sacred head, once wounded)

Tune: Lux Eoi, 8,7,8,7,8,7,8,7. (Alleluia, alleluiah, Hearts to Heaven..)

Tune: Praise my soul, 8,7,8,7,8,7. (Praise, my soul, the king of heaven)

Tune: Hollingside, 7s, Double. (Jesu, lover of my soul)

Tune: Miles Lane, C.M., 8,6,8,6. (All hail the power of Jesus' name)

Tune: Evangelists, 8,8,7,8,8,7. (Come, pure hearts in sweetest measure)

Tune: Dominus Regit Me, 8,7,8,7. (The King of love my Shepherd is)

Tune: Saviour, like a Shepherd, 8,7,8,7,4,4,7. (Saviour, like a shepherd lead us)

Tune: Darwall's 148th, 12,12,8,8. (Ye holy angels bright)

Tune: Love Divine, 8,7,8,7,8,7,8,7. (Love divine, all loves excelling)

Tune: Bread of Heaven, 7s. (Bread of Heaven, on thee we feed)

Tune: Chrysostom, 8s. (Jesu, my Lord, my God, my all)

Tune: Cross of Jesus, 8,7,8,7. (Come, thou long-expected Jesus)

Tune: Abends, L.M., 8s. Glory to thee, my God, this night)

Tune: Gerontius, C.M., 8,6,8,6. (Praise to the Holiest in the height)

Tune: St. Clement, 9,8,9,8. (The day Thou gavest, Lord, is ended)

Tune: O Galilee! L.M., 8s. (Jesus shall reign where'er the sun)

INDEX OF FIRST LINES

The numbers in brackets are the hymn numbers in the Arabic Language Hymn Book.

A noble person stands alone 99 (260)

A precious name, sublime, ever 122 (313)

A sound rang forth in the highest 38 (93)

Above a spacious sea of glass 86 (222)

At the break of day one morning 50 (132)

At the right time this life shall cease 83 (209)

Be not sad and troubled in mind 95 (245)

Behold, morning has appeared 16 (33)

Behold, the Lord Jesus had said 120 (311)

Believers have waited too long 34 (85)

Bestower of the guiding light 71 (171)

Blessed are the people who slept 84 (213)

Blessed be that majesty 2 (5)

Blind son of Timaeus 138 (406)

Bow down to our Creator Lord 3 (6)

By the word of the most high One 81 (196)

Christ has gained the kingship truly 58 (148)

Christ shall come, His promise keeping 33 (83)

Come, believers, to His body 80 (195)

Come O Sinners, repent quickly 102 (266)

Come on, come on, approach closely 101 (263)

Come promptly to Christ Jesus the Lord 97 (254)

Come to the Redeemer 125 (320)

Consoling Spirit, ever gleaming 68 (166)

Dear Lord, grant us this eventide 18 (37)

Faithful Shepherd, hear our prayer 23 (47)

For the day of passing I earnestly long 86 (221)

From most trustworthy Jesus 106 (275)

Give me a heart, both pure and clean 64 (159)

Glory to God the mighty One 6 (11)

God is a Spirit of great might 24 (53)

God is love, so Heaven and earth 93 (238)

God's Son and Son of man 76 (183)

Gracious Father, for whom we wait 75 (178)

Guide my soul, O Jesus, Lord 115 (296)

He shall come, our faithful Saviour 32 (82)

His crown was braided with thorns 47 (121)

His the authority 8 (18)

How right that our eyes should 103 (267)

I cannot proceed on the way 109 (282)

I dedicate myself 82 (206)

I have a book from my Lord God 29 (75)

I have obtained peace from my Lord 133 (354)

I love the Lord, but not to gain 134 (355)

I love to distance myself from 22 (51)

I offer You, O Lord on high 123 (316)

I pray with thanks most readily 13 (27)

I was chained by iniquity 140 (434)

I was in the prison of sin 78 (191)

If calamities assail me 110 (283)

If Christ had not loved me, undone 92 (237)

If I walk in the wilderness 129 (343)

If in the Saviour you grow old 135 (358)

If my soul, stained with sin 126 (321)

If the days of my trial run no more 89 (225)

If the righteousness of people 79 (193)

If we sailed the waves of the sea 127 (341)

Increase Your love to me 132 (351)

It is finished, the Lord had said 43 (116)

Jesus my Lord approached sinners with love 139 (417)

Jesus, my Saviour, wondrous One 41 (111)

Jesus, You obeyed Your Father's instruction 42 (117)

Like the bright star that guided 39 (98)

Lo! Christ comes and rather quickly 35 (86)

Lord Jesus, You loved us lifelong 91 (232)

Lord, you are my peace and ark 111 (286)

My heart loves my great Beloved 77 (195)

My heart's hope and my life's light 130 (349)

My soul, arise and praise 9 (21)

My soul in the arms of Jesus 112 (287)

My soul, praise the Lord and never 94 (241)

My soul will be at peace if I 104 (271)

Night fell and its curtains scattered 46 (120)

O beloved Friend of mine 107 (276)

O beloved Jesus 66 (164)

O brilliant and splendid Light 119 (30)

O Father, merciful and good 14 (30)

O forgiving Redeemer 124 (317)

O Guardian of the vast universe 128 (342)

O Holy Spirit of the most high God 61 (155)

O Jesus, Lord of peace, see how 28 (72)

O Jesus, my rock and bliss 105 (274)

O King of the world, and head 121 (307)

O lonesome Sleeper 67 (165)

O Lord Christ, be to me indeed 113 (288)

O Lord, giver of strength and might 72 (172)

O most loving who died instead of mankind 100 (264)

O my God and Master, pity my sad plight 114 (291)

O my Soul, arise and bless the Lord 11 (25)

O my Soul, rise up hurriedly 15 (32)

O Nations of the earth, arise 36 (88)

O Pilgrims upon the way 88 (223)

O Spirit, consoling Spirit 65 (161)

O Spirit that ever glows 62 (156)

On the throne of our Redeemer 56 (146)

Planet of the morning, glow 116 (297)

Praise the Creator of the worlds 70 (168)

Praise the Lord, praise Him mightily 7 (15)

Rise, believers, fight corruption 136 (384)

Rise, my soul, and seek your part 90 (226)

Rise O Singer and sing the name 59 (151)

She hurried to the tomb, her Jesus seeking 53 (136)

Should my night descend upon me 60 (153)

Sinner, have you heard it once more? 63 (157)

Take me by the hand, lead me 118 (301)

Thank God whose favour overflows 10 (23)

Thanking Your holy name, our theme 12 (26)

The Christ is risen today 51 (133)

The host of Heaven came singing 37 (89)

The host of Heaven descended 48 (127)

The light of morn in eastern skies 17 (34)

The Lord has brought us in peace 20 (43)

The Lord has gone out of sight 55 (143)

The Saviour was hung up high 44 (118)

The sign of the cross is in place 73 (176)

The soul's enemy draws his sword 137 (386)

The sun has travelled with us 21 (44)

The universe is but a page 31 (81)

The words of the Lord [ill the heart 30 (76)

There is no sweeter name 25 (59)

There was joy and great rejoicing 49 (131)

To God who from eternity 4 (7,8,9)

To a dark and dim grave 52 (134)

To the merciful One 1 (1)

To your beloved Redeemer 96 (252)

Today He calls us, whose great love 98 (261)

Total sovereignty is Yours 45 (119)

Upon the hills of Bethlehem 40 (99)

Upon the Saviour's brow there shines 57 (147)

We come to place this body in the soil 85 (214)

We praise Him who fills all in all 5 (10)

What a sublime sight, by greatness attended 54 (138)

When the darkness enshrouds my soul 131 (350)

Who helps the held and weary 108 (279)

We give to God our utmost praise 69 (167)

When the day's sun goes to sleep 19 (38)

Wish I could settle at the feet 27 (64)

Yearned for Spirit of life, our rock 117 (299)

Your eyes, O great exalted Lord 26 (62)

You said, O Lord, when on this earth 74 (177)

www.ingramcontent.com/pod-product-compliance
Lightning Source LLC
Chambersburg PA
CBHW070350120526
44590CB00014B/1073